THUNDERBOLT THE FALCON

THUNDERBOLT
the
FALCON

By

C.K. Thompson, R.A.O.U., J.P.

(Member of the Royal Australasian Ornithologists' Union and the
Royal Zoological Society of N.S.W.)

This edition published 2017
By Living Book Press
147 Durren Rd, Jilliby, 2259
Copyright © The Estate of C.K. Thompson, 1950

Cover image from maxpixel.freegreatpicture.com

The publisher would like to give a huge 'Thank You' to the author's family
for their assistance in making this book available once more.

National Library of Australia Cataloguing-in-Publication entry:

Creator:	Thompson, C.K. (Charles Kenneth), 1904-1980 author
Title:	Thunderbolt the falcon / C. K. Thompson.
ISBN:	9780648104834 (paperback)
Target Audience:	For primage school age.
Subjects:	Peregrine falcon--Juvenile fiction.
	Falcons--Juvenile fiction.

AUTHOR'S NOTE

This, primarily, is a story of one of our noblest and most courageous birds of prey, the peregrine falcon, and the efforts of two lads to train one as a hunting hawk.

Australia is rich in unique fauna—animals and birds that are found nowhere else in the world—but our great country must share the peregrine with almost every other part of the globe. That being so, I have ventured in this book to link the sunny Australian bushland of today with the ancient forests of mediaeval Europe where, centuries long past, kings, princes, barons, bishops, lords, knights, and even their fair ladies, practised the art of falconry, an art that today is practically obsolete.

The birthplace of falconry is lost in the mists of antiquity, for it is thousands of years old. The sport flourished among the early Britons in England during the Roman occupation and among the Saxons, particularly in the reign of King Ethelbert (760 A.O.).

Falconry was the major pastime in England from the Norman Conquest up to the end of the 17th century, and it is interesting to note the stringent and oppressive laws passed in early England regarding the sport. Under the Normans the privilege of owning hawks was reserved for people of the highest rank. Anyone transgressing this law was promptly dealt with in a fashion that precluded him from indulging again in any kind of sport, except, possibly, rising from the grave and haunting his oppressors.

Though hawking with birds has practically died out in England, it is still fairly popular in some Eastern countries and just prior to World War II it had quite a vogue in parts of the United States. There have been spasmodic attempts to popularise it in Australia, but it has never taken on.

In the running narrative of this book I have described in some detail the method used to train falcons for hawking, so if any reader feels like catching a bird and then has the time and patience to "give it a fly," by all means let him do so.

My authority for hawks attacking model aeroplanes is the Model Aero Club of Newcastle, N.S.W., which from time to time has reported the bringing down of free-flying planes by these birds of prey. Hawks have dived on the models and then retired, puzzled, only to return again if the model kept on flying. Several have been grounded in this fashion.

In conclusion, I would like to mention that the episode in which a performer was rolled up in the curtain at a school concert and some gentle humorist freed a box of mice among the audience, really occurred, many years ago. I was in the audience and witnessed the lot.

C. K. THOMPSON.

Contents

CHAPTER ONE

A Pair of Peregrines

HIGH up the side of a precipitous rocky cliff in a deep crevice hollowed out by time and weather, a pair of peregrine falcons had built their nest of sticks and twigs lined with soft bark, bits of wool and stray feathers. The sticks and twigs were collected from the summit of the cliff itself, while the bits of wool had come from fences and stumps against which idle sheep, grazing in paddocks, had rubbed their fleecy hides. The stray feathers had once belonged to certain pathetic victims of the predatory falcons.

For Black-cheek the falcon and Tiercel her mate were killers: the fastest, strongest and most fearless of all the Australian hawks. They were up before daylight hunting and they were still at it when the last rays of the setting sun heralded the darkness that brought safety, or at least a breathing space, to their potential victims.

The two falcons were proud of their nest, which was their own, unaided work. Unlike their cousins the kestrels, the sparrow-hawks, the kites and certain other birds that made shift with the deserted nests of crows and ravens in high trees, the peregrines always built their own homes. Second-hand dwellings were beneath their dignity.

Just above the crevice in which their nest had been built, a gnarled and twisted gum tree jutted from the face of the cliff. How it obtained enough sustenance to live in that rocky eminence was a secret of Mother Nature; but it was a puzzle that did not bother the falcons. They were content that it was there, because from its few scraggy branches they could obtain a panoramic view of the whole of the vast open country spread out before them.

They were a handsome pair of birds, those peregrines. Blue-grey backs, black heads and cheeks, whitish throats and fine barrings on their breasts made a combination of colour that was most attractive—except to the birds and small animals they hunted.

There were very few birds upon which Black-cheek and Tiercel did not prey. They took their victims as they came from ducks to larks; and there was quite a number of human pigeon-fanciers who had cause to regret the existence of the peregrines when their treasured racing birds failed to return to their home lofts. The falcons also enjoyed rabbits, particularly young ones.

A proverb that Black-cheek and Tiercel could have adopted as their family motto was "the early bird catches the worm"—but with the substitution of something much more attractive and satisfying than the worm. The falcons were not interested in worms but they were definitely in favour of early starting times.

It was their invariable custom to leave their roosting place when there was just enough light for them to see what they were doing. Sometimes they hunted together, but quite often they went their separate ways, one not caring what the other did.

Both were very wise and experienced birds. They started to hunt at daybreak because at that hour most other birds were still asleep or only half awake on their roosts. This was a good thing for Black-cheek and Tiercel who, cruising slowly among the open trees with deadly keen eyes raking the twigs, leaves and branches, often picked up early breakfasts. Balls of feathers huddled in sleep never knew what happened to them, for the falcons struck like lightning, the victims dying violently without the least chance to escape. Occasionally, however, a luckless parakeet, snatched off its perch and carried away in the fierce clutch of the falcon's talons, screamed its dying protests until the slayer, irritated by the noise, landed with it on a convenient branch or on the ground and made short work of it. Black-cheek had been known even to make a meal in mid-air.

Out in the centre of a paddock some miles from their nest there stood a long-dead tree with one lonely branch. The trunk was straight up and on the very top of this Black-cheek had her favourite spotting perch. Tiercel generally occupied the lone branch, which was ten feet below. This was their chosen hunting area for, apart from the bushes and trees from which small birds could be taken, rabbits were plentiful. Both falcons liked rabbits very much, especially kittens. From their lofty lookout they could easily locate the unwary young animals and in their fast powerdives they rarely missed. The victim secured, it was always carried away to an open place and devoured on the ground.

Black-cheek and Tiercel built their nest in early August, beating most other birds to it by some weeks. Their young ones would be ready to hunt when the nesting season of other birds was in full swing. Nestlings provided an easy harvest for young falcons not yet fully experienced in the art of taking their victims on the wing.

Black-cheek had laid three eggs in the nest in the crevice in the cliff. They were buff-colored and covered all over with reddish-brown marks. Only two hatched, both female birds, and hungry young eyasses they were.

It was not, of course, the first family of Black-cheek and Tiercel. Several broods had been raised and sent forth into the world by the two falcons. In between breeding seasons they did not always keep together. They were wanderers, these peregrines, as their name implies, and though neither strayed very far outside a ten miles' radius of their nesting place, sometimes they did not see each other for weeks on end. Often they hunted singly and often in pairs; but when they were together, occasionally they did not even prey as a combined team but went into independent action when game was sighted.

Though Black-cheek and Tiercel sometimes strayed to the

coast and sometimes inland, their decided preference was for the heavily-timbered and rugged mountainous country. Bold and fearless and in flight easily the strongest of all the Australian hawks, excepting, of course, their giant kinsman, the wedge-tailed eagle, the peregrines preyed on anything and everything.

Black-cheek was by far the larger bird. She was twenty inches in length and had a wing-span of something over three feet. Tiercel was shorter in body by fully five inches and his wing-span was not quite three feet. In flight, both were swift and undulating, their long, pointed wings capable of deep, powerful strokes, propelling them through the air as fast as they desired to travel. And though their deep but wheezy call, kra-kra-kra, when hunting, was enough to strike fear into the boldest of birds, it was nothing to the terror their harsh scream created when they threw themselves into their swift killing swoop.

The two eyasses, as young falcons are called, grew apace. They were like their parents in appearance, having similar black heads and cheeks and white throats, also blue-grey backs, but whereas the adult birds had fine barrings on their breasts, the eyasses were marked with broad stripes. As they grew older, these would give way to the barrings of their parents.

When the young falcons were old enough to leave the nest, they stayed for some time on a narrow rocky platform which jutted out in front of the nest crevice. Six feet above their heads was a branch of the gnarled and twisted gum tree which their parents used as a look-out. And it was from the platform to this branch that they each made their first uncertain flights.

As time passed, Black-cheek and Tiercel conducted their offspring down out of the hills and over to the paddock in which their other look-out was situated-the long-dead tree with the one lonely branch and the bare top. Here, perched side by side on the branch, the eyasses watched their parents hunting and learned a lot. Naturally they were most eager to join in the hunt, but they were told sternly to stay where they were and their food would be brought to them. In the meantime, between snacks, they were to watch their parents and pay strict attention to what was going on. And they did so.

The old birds adopted a technique that was easy for the eyasses to follow. On leaving the tree, both birds soared up and up to about one hundred feet, keen eyes raking the ground. Suddenly Tiercel saw a half-grown rabbit emerge from a burrow near an acacia bush and sit in the mouth of it. Like an arrow from a bow he threw himself into his power-dive and flashed earthwards. Black-cheek watched his progress with a keen, professional eye and saw him spoil things by screaming harshly when within a few yards of the rabbit. Quick as Tiercel was, the bunny was quicker, and though terrified, it had just sufficient wits to tumble into its burrow, out of which Tiercel had no hope of dragging it.

Black-cheek soared upwards and circled and then became aware of something still higher. She did not know what it was except that it was a bird of some kind. The sound of wing-beats of course told her that. In a wide upward spiral, she projected herself above what turned out to be a large blue crane.

This slow-moving bird had been fishing in the swamp a few miles away and was now making its way to a small creek where it hoped to get a feed of fresh-water yabbies. If it knew of the presence of the falcon it made no sign but continued on its way, uttering its loud, creaking call and flapping its big wings as if it were sheer hard work to do so.

Black-cheek easily followed its flight, circling high above it. She did this while the crane flew about fifty yards and then suddenly tipped over and fell downwards. With a harsh and savage scream she struck the unfortunate crane on the neck with one of her talons and sent it tumbling to earth. It was dead before it hit the ground and seconds afterwards Black-cheek was tearing away the feathers preparatory to making a meal.

Black-cheek was lunching quietly when suddenly she paused and cocked her head on one side. She had heard something. Leaving the body of the crane she shot into the air and took by surprise a graceful little Nankeen kestrel that had been hovering overhead. The kestrel took to its wings and fled. Black-cheek did not follow it but dropped back to earth to resume her interrupted meal. She had had absolutely nothing to fear from the kestrel either as a mealstealer or an antagonist, but she didn't want the other bird around.

Nankeen kestrel was a relation of Black-cheek's but a very different type of bird. Known generally as the sparrowhawk possibly because it hovered for long periods with rapidly beating wings looking for its prey, it fed mostly on grasshoppers, crickets, small reptiles, mice and sometimes the young of ground-nesting birds.

Black-cheek had plenty of relations and except for Grey Falcon, which was a rather timid bird and slower in its flight than the other falcons, all of the peregrine's relatives were swift and tireless slayers.

Take Little Falcon for example. Here was a small kinsman of which the peregrine might well be proud. Its laboured flight and awkward hovering with rapidly-beating wings when searching for food was a snare and a delusion for, the game in sight, it was as swift as a dart and, taking into consideration its size, was as bold, if not bolder, than some of its larger relations.

Black Falcon, which, when fully grown, was about the size of a crow, was another hawk to be treated with the greatest respect. Swift on the wing like the rest of the family, its favourite sport was hunting quail and larks, soaring and diving on them from a great height. It also preyed upon any other bird which was unfortunate enough to encounter it in open country, dealing with its victims in the same ungentle manner as its peregrine cousin. It was a vecy dark brown bird, almost black, thus bearing a close resemblance to Brown Hawk. But Brown Hawk preferred to pounce on any small birds to which he took a fancy instead of seizing them in the air. In addition, he did not despise a meal of beetles, caterpillars or mice. A bit of a comedian, at times he indulged in aerial acrobatics, flying erratically and doing flips and side slips like a stunting aeroplane pilot.

But Brown Hawk was not such a stunt artist as Crested Hawk, who, after soaring to a great height, often fell earthwards like a tumbler pigeon, whistling loud and clear as he did so. Crested Hawk, a most graceful bird, was not a killer. He lived mainly on insects, but blotted his copybook by occasionally dining off a dead animal.

Collared Sparrowhawk, a kinsman of Nankeen Kestrel, was a true "sparrow-hawk." A lively little chap, he lived almost wholly upon small birds.

Black-cheek's other relations included the goshawks, the kites and the harriers, all of which competed with each other for food. Among her larger kinsmen were the little eagles, the sea eagles, the ospreys, the buzzards and, noblest of them all, the mighty wedged-tailed eagle.

Neither Black-cheek nor Tiercel had any family pride in so far as their hawk relations were concerned. The law of the wild laid down survival of the fittest. The peregrines attended strictly to their own business and that, at the moment, was the training of and subsequent launching into the feathered world of their lusty eyasses. The survival of the fittest! If the youngsters could not stand up for their own rights and wrest a good living from the bush, the mountains and the plains after they had outgrown their home ties, then so much the worse for them. Their parents would not care; they had their own lives to live.

But the eyasses were apt pupils, the fierce children of fierce predatory parents and they could face the future with full confidence.

CHAPTER TWO

Introducing a Knightly Sport

NOT a great distance from the paddock in which stood the old dead tree taken over by Black-cheek and Tiercel as their watch-tower, was the modest home of young Joe McKenzie and his parents. Joe's father was a timbergetter and, consequently, a very hard worker. Young Joe, like most boys, liked work about as much as he enjoyed going to school or washing his feet. He was, however, a great reader of books, mainly of the adventure type, but he was rather conservative in his choice.

In this modern age when small boys think more of spaceships and interplanetary travel, mowing down Martians with ray guns and disintegrating demons from Venus with hydrogen pistols, Joe stuck stolidly to the six-gun in fancy and the catapult in reality. Let others blast whole planets to smithereens with ultra-atomic artillery if they liked. A pair of six-shooters in the hands of Billy the Kid or Bloodstained Basil terrorising a western American cowtown gave him all the thrills he wanted. For one thing, cowboys and Indians, cattle rustlers and the Wild West actually existed, whereas the authenticity of life on the other planets has yet to be established.

It was his inability to procure the latest Buffalo Bill novel during his last trip into the township that had driven him to read the book he now had.

Wandering restlessly around the house and disdaining to attend to certain small jobs listed for him by his mother before she left home that morning to spend the day with her married sister, Joe saw the book lying on the floor in a corner. Using it as a football, he sent it flying across the room, shedding a few leaves in flight. It was an ancient and battered volume with only one cover, which bore in very faded lettering the austere title, "Flower of Knighthood." It had been lying around the house for as long as Joe could remember. It had been used in its time as a doorstop and a prop to keep a window open. He had seen his father tear pages out of it to use as spills to light his pipe from the fire. As far as he knew, neither of his parents had ever read it. He himself had never even thought of it.

Then, in sheer desperation, he decided to give it a go, so, retrieving it from under the kitchen sink, he mooched out into the yard and settled himself under the shade of a tree.

Joe did not expect to derive much instruction or enjoyment from the battered volume. He yawned before he even opened it. He noted that the first seven pages were missing and when he glanced at the end to see how the story finished, discovered that the last eighteen pages were not there. Ah, well, he told himself philosophically, there might be something worthwhile in the middle of the thing.

There was. And that something, strangely enough, had a most important bearing, not only upon the future careers of a pair of peregrine falcons at that moment lunching off a small rabbit in the paddock over the way, but upon another falcon as yet unborn.

Though he had to commence the story in mid-air as it were, Joe soon grasped the fact that it was set in the reign of King Edward III, when knights, yeomen and scurvy knaves rushed around with bows and arrows and went forth to battle in tin suits. The only firearms Edward and his men appeared to possess were things called bombards—very primitive cannon which fired iron balls a few yards or so. That is, when they behaved themselves. Mostly it seemed that they exploded when fired, blowing themselves to bits and killing everyone on their own side within a radius of a hundred yards.

Joe grunted and felt inclined to throw the book away. After all, it was historical tripe and he got enough of that at school. He read a few more pages and was thus engaged when he received a visitor. This was a small boy with fair hair and a dreamy expression on a face the main feature of which was a snub nose. He wore a dirty shirt and had a hole in the seat of his pants—standard uniform for all Joe McKenzie's mates. He did not announce his arrival in the accepted social fashion. Instead, the dreamy expression still on his face, he stooped down silently, collected a large pebble and shied it at Joe. The pebble landed on the back of that earnest reader's head, causing him to suspend his literary researches and emit a sharp howl.

"What are you reading, Joe?" asked the visitor mildly.

"You silly looking Pommy coot!" howled Joe, rubbing the back of his head. "What the dickens do you think you're up to, donging me like that with a dirty big rock. A man ought to drop you."

"Drop me, huh? And where can you get ten men in a hurry to help you?" asked the newcomer, young David Burton. "Don't lose your excitement, Joe. And by the way, if you don't knock off calling me a Pommy, I'll drop you, not you drop me."

"Well, you are a Pommy, ain't you?" snorted the aggrieved Joe. "Coming here and pelting me with huge rocks. Why didn't you stay in England?"

"Too many bombs around," replied David cheerfully.

In spite of the rather rough greetings exchanged, these two boys were the very best of friends. David Burton had come to Australia as a baby with his mother towards the end of World War II, and they now lived with his grandfather in a cottage not very far from Joe's home. David's father had been one of the heroes of the Battle of Britain and later had been shot down in action during a bombing raid over Berlin. When his wife had migrated to Australia with her young son David, her father, old John Mannering, had come with them. Joe and David had become firm friends from their very first meeting. Joe rarely used the insulting name "Pommy" when referring to David unless he was particularly annoyed and even then there was no real sting in the epithet, as David knew.

"What are you reading, Joe?" the English boy repeated. "That doesn't look much like a cowboy yarn."

"It isn't," said Joe as David dropped to a seat on the ground at his side. "It is a book about knights and other balmy jokers when Edward the Third was King of England."

"Oh, history tripe?" asked David in disgust. "Chuck the thing away and let us go shooting birds with our catapults. Come on."

"That's a good idea, Dave," nodded Joe. "But there are bits of this yarn that have got me tricked. You come from England, so you ought to know all about it. Help me out."

"Here, break it down!" protested David. "I come from England all right, but I wasn't knocking around in the reign of Edward III. Better see Grandfather. He saw out the reigns of Edward VII and Edward VIII, the bloke who is now Duke of Windsor. Will that do you?"

"Oh, don't be a bigger goat than you have to," begged Joe. He paused and snorted. Then, "From what I can make out so far in this yarn, this joker Edward the Third wasn't satisfied with owning England, but wanted to clout on France too and be king of both. The French birds objected, so Edward the Third carted an army to France, also his son, a bit of a prawn about 16 years old, and also an Aboriginal."

"An Aboriginal?" exclaimed David. "What do you mean, an Aboriginal?"

"Well, it says here that he was called the Black Prince," Joe pointed out seriously.

"Stone the crows, he wasn't an Aboriginal," laughed David. "He was called the Black Prince because he always wore black armour."

"Is that so? Well, anyway, there was a lot of swordfighting and arrow-shooting at some joint or other in France called Crecy, where this Aboriginal, I mean, this Black Prince joker, won a pair of spurs. That is one part that has me tricked. It doesn't say how he won 'em, whether in a raffle or playing cards or what."

"They were knight's spurs," put in David.

"So what? I don't care a continental red cent if he wore them in the daytime. That's not the point at all. This Black Prince joker was given part of the army to command by his old man and looked like collecting the father of a belting off the Froggies. Somebody stuck his beak in—some earl or duke-by telling the old man—Edward the Third, I mean—that his silly son was copping a rough trot and he'd better hop in and help him or England would be short one Black Prince, also a few thousand archers and knights; and he himself would probably do in his chances of swiping the crown of France."

Here Joe paused for a few seconds and rapidly thumbed through the pages of the book.

"Listen to this, Dave," he went on. "'When the noble told the king that the Black Prince needed assistance, the royal Edward III replied proudly, "No. Let the boy win his spurs."' I don't get it, Dave, do you? You'd think it was a battle he wanted to win, not a pair of rusty old spurs which he could buy in any second-hand shop; or, if he wasn't too fussy, could pinch off a dead soldier."

Joe McKenzie, it would seem, had little conception of, or regard for, the ancient laws and usages of chivalry.

"You've got it all twisted, Joe," said David scornfully. "The king meant that the Black Prince had to win his spurs of knighthood-that he had to prove his bravery as a true knight."

"Well, it all sounds so dashed silly to me," said Joe. "A prince is much higher than a knight, isn't he? Right. Now, if this Aboriginal prince was already a prince, what the heck was the sense or use of his winning knight's spurs? I mean to say, he was sliding down the scale a bit, wasn't he? And apart from all else, couldn't he have got a pair of blessed spurs from his old man for nix without having to go and fight a war against the French fellers?"

"He was born a prince but that didn't make him a brave knight," said David patiently. "In those days a man had to prove he was brave. He had to win his spurs by heroic deeds on the battlefield. Then, if he were of gentle birth or noble blood, he became a knight. There were even cases of ordinary soldiers being knighted for outstanding services to the king and the country. In these days they make anybody a knight whether he is brave or not."

"All right, all right, don't give me a lecture," said Joe impatiently. "Just kindly explain to me how a prince who is higher than a duke, an earl, a lord, or a knight, wanted to become a knight by winning a pair of spurs? It's all haywire and whangdoodle."

"The spurs were made of gold and were the badge of knighthood, just like a returned soldier gets an R.S.L. badge when he joins the Returned Soldiers' League. Your old man has one, so you ought to know that," said David.

"Oh," said Joe, light breaking on him. "But that doesn't explain about a prince wanting to be disrated to a knight."

"Oh, for heaven's sake," exclaimed David. "A knight really meant a brave man. If the Black Prince was a coward, he'd still be a prince, but not a true knight. Do you get it now?"

"No," said Joe.

David saw that it was plain useless trying to explain the niceties of chivalry to the earthbound Joe and he was not going to try any more.

"It's all as mad as a snake," said Joe.

"Too silly for words," agreed David.

"Absolutely ratbag," added Joe.

"Plain daft and the height of stupidity," supplemented David. What was the use?

There was silence for a moment or two as Joe idly turned the pages of the battered volume to look at the illustrations. One caught his eye. It was the picture of a knight dressed in the fashionable attire of the day, sitting on a horse with a bird perched on his gloved wrist.

"Wonder what this goat is up to?" Joe grunted.

"Give me a look. What does it say underneath the picture?" asked David.

"Edward III was a great lover of falconry. In between battles in France he went hawking with his knights,' " read Joe.

"A lot of nobles did it in the Middle Ages." remarked David.

"Did what?"

"Went out hawking" said David.

"Hawking? Hawking what?" demanded Joe, squinting at the illustration. "Don't tell me he was trying to sell that parrot squatting on his fist! He must have been pretty hard up to go around hawking parrots like a drunk hawking bootlaces on a street corner! Still, I guess wars cost a lot of dough. All the same, he wouldn't raise much by selling flea-bitten parrots, would he?"

"That's not a parrot, Joe, you silly goat. It's a falcon," exclaimed David. "Stone the wombats, don't you know anything?"

"I know enough to lay you flat on your back if you get too cheeky, young Dave" said Joe darkly. "Anyway, what is a falcon?"

"It's a kind of hawk. In England the kings, earls and knights used to train them to hunt other birds."

"Look, don't let us get on that knight argument again," begged Joe. "Anyway, how did they train them?"

"They got them young in the nest and taught them. Then they took the birds into the fields and set them on to other birds. The falcons chased the birds and caught them for their masters. A bit like greyhound dogs are trained to hunt hares and rabbits."

"Well, what do you know about that!" exclaimed Joe with great animation. "Say, what a great lurk that would be! Wish I had lived in those days! I'll bet I'd have had the best trained falcon in the world."

"Naturally!" murmured David in a tone which made Joe look at him suspiciously. David's face, however, was an innocent blank.

"I wonder if any of the hawks we have here in Australia could be trained to hunt birds?" asked Joe after a few moments' deep thought. He heaved a regretful sigh. "Guess not. Anyway, even if they were trainable, I suppose nobody would know how to do it now. I'll bet nobody has trained a hawk or a falcon for hundreds of years."

"Now that is where you are wrong, as usual, young Joseph," said David. "My grandfather says that there is still a lot of it done—in England, China, India and America. He did it himself when he was a lad."

"Don't give me that line of tripe," scoffed the doubting Joe.

"It's a fact. Grandfather Mannering used to be a gamekeeper on the estates of the Earl of Rockvale in England and he knows all there is to know about falcons and hawks and so on. I'll bet, too, that he knows as much about Australian birds as he does about those in England. He is always out in the bush watching and studying them."

"Gosh!" breathed Joe. He was entranced with the vision he had conjured up. "I wonder if he would tell us how to train a hawk? But I don't suppose he knows anything about it, in spite of what you say."

"There is one sure way to prove that," said David. "You come over to our place and have a yarn with him. I don't know if any of the Australian hawks can be trained, but if they can, grandfather will know. Of course, whether he would train one for you or show you how it is done, is a bird of a different feather."

"Clever coot, aren't you? Bird of a different feather!" said Joe.

He jumped to his feet, hurled the book into the nearby fowlyard, nearly skittling a half-grown duck, and announced himself as being ready to make the pilgrimage to the Burton home.

"What, straight away?" asked David. "I thought we were going out shooting with our shanghais?"

"That can wait. We can go shooting any old time," said Joe. "Let's go and see what your dopey grandfather knows about training hawks."

CHAPTER THREE

Grandfather Mannering

WHEN David and Joe arrived at the Burton home, old Mr. Mannering was not there. David's mother told them that he had not yet returned from his usual daily stroll around the bush. Mr. Mannering was a great lover of nature and spent a lot of his time studying birds and animals.

It was ten minutes before he arrived home and he was full of his experiences. It seemed that he had been sitting for hours on the bank of the creek watching a pair of birds build a nest.

"Clever little chaps they were, too," he told Joe and David. "Little diamond birds, or rather pardalotes. Do you know that these wee birds actually dig a long tunnel in a bank and build their nests in complete darkness at the end of the tunnel?"

"I've seen 'em," said Joe. "Pretty little spotted jokers. What did you say their name was? I always called 'em Johnny Banker."

"As good a name as their real one," said Grandfather.

Joe, assisted a little by David, then told the old man the reason for their deputation to him.

"It was my idea, Mr. Mannering," Joe confessed. "I thought it would be pretty exciting if we could train up a hawk to catch other birds. It would beat shooting 'em with catapults and guns, or trapping them."

"Well, now, Joe," said the old man with a chuckle, "I haven't seen any hawking since I was a young man. I was then assistant gamekeeper to my old dad. He knew all about falconry. The Earl of Rockvale was one of the very few English gentry who went hawking with falcons. It is hundreds of years since falconry was an organised sport in the Old Country, but the Rockvale family kept it up as a sort of tradition. They have a falcon in their family crest and away back in the days of Edward the Third, the then Earl of Rockvale owned the grand champion falcon of England."

"Looks as if we will never get away from this Edward the Third joker," said Joe gloomily.

"The Mannering family has been in the service of the Rockvales, father and son, for centuries, and it was part of their work to train falcons. But that is all over and done with now."

"How is that?" Joe wanted to know.

"When the old earl died, the title died with him," Mr. Mannering explained. "He had only one child, a daughter, and the authorities could not trace any male heir to succeed to the title, so the peerage became extinct. The daughter was not interested in falconry. When my dad died, I became head gamekeeper and when I retired a few years ago my son Henry—he is young David's uncle—took over from me and is still at Rockvale Manor as gamekeeper for Lady Margaret Candish's family. She is the daughter of the last earl, as I told you."

"Do you think we could learn how to train hawks to catch birds, Mr. Mannering?" asked the eager Joe. "What would be the best birds to train?"

"The best bird for hawking is the peregrine falcon," the old man said decisively.

"Don't think I've ever seen one," said Joe doubtfully.

"Oh, they are around," said Grandfather. "I've seen them myself. Of course they are not common birds, but they're about."

"What, here in Australia?" exclaimed David and Joe in chorus.

"Right here in this very district," assented Mr. Mannering. "The peregrine falcon is a bird that gets about. Why, his very name, peregrine, comes from the Latin word peregrinus, which means 'wandering.' You'll find him all over Europe, Asia and Africa. In

America they call him the duck-hawk. Out here in Australia he is known as the black-cheeked falcon and he is undoubtedly the strongest and swiftest of all the Australian hawks."

Old Mr. Mannering suddenly smiled.

"If you lads are toying with the idea of training falcons for hunting, you had better forget it. Apart from the fact that it is a long, tedious business, there is the matter of strict hawking tradition to consider," he said gravely, the twinkle in his eye giving the lie to the gravity of his tones.

"Meaning what?" demanded Joe.

"I said just now that the best hawk for hunting is the peregrine falcon," the old man replied. "Actually that is not quite correct. The gyrfalcon is probably superior. We can forget all about that bird, however, because it is a native of Scandinavia.

"But I am straying from the point. The ancient laws of falconry were very strict about what type of hawk a man could possess. There were very heavy penalties in the days of old when knights were bold imposed upon a person who trained a bird outside his station in life."

"I don't get that," said Joe. "What was that in aid of?"

"Just conforming to the precedence of nobility. And remember, it was the law of England. It laid down that the eagle, vulture and merloun were for an emperor, the gyrfalcon and its tiercel for a king, the falcon gentle and its tiercel for a prince, the falcon of the rock for a duke, the peregrine falcon for an earl, the buzzard for a baron, the sacre and sacret for a knight, the lanner and lanneret for an esquire, the merlin for a lady, the hobby for a young man, the goshawk for a yeoman, the goshawk tiercel for a poor man, the sparrow-hawk for a priest and the kestrel for a knave, or servant."

"Holy wars!" ejaculated Joe. "What the dickens is all this merloun, sacre, lanneret and tiercel business?"

"Different types of hawks in England in those days. Some of them still exist. But a tiercel is the male bird of the species."

"What's he called that for?" asked Joe in some bewilderment.

"The name tiercel comes from a Latin word meaning 'third.' There is an old saying among falconers that the third egg of a falcon always produces a male bird."

"And is it right?"

"I have never been able to prove it," smiled Grandfather.

Joe brooded intensely for a moment or two while Mr. Mannering looked at him in amusement. "Seems to me," said the boy at last, "that as I'm not in that list, all I get is the crow."

"Crow!" exclaimed Grandfather. "I'm afraid that you would not do much good trying to train a crow to hunt."

Joe gave a guffaw of mirth.

"I didn't mean that I'd go hunting with a crow," he laughed. "That is a good Aussie saying—getting the crow. It means getting the worse end of the stick."

"Getting the crow is getting the worse end of the stick," repeated Grandfather gravely. "I'm afraid I don't understand. Seems to me I'll never learn all the queer Australian expressions before I pass on. How can getting a crow give you a stick?"

"I think the crow business comes from an old bush story," said Joe. "At least, my dad says so. The story runs that a bushman and an aborigine were out shooting one day and they dropped a duck and a crow between them. The bushman said to the abo, 'Well, Jacky, now we'll divide up the bag. You can have first pick. Will you take the crow and leave me the duck, or will I take the duck and let you have the crow?' Jacky scratched his nut and replied, 'I dunno. Seems to me, boss, that I get the blessed crow all the time!'"

The old man laughed heartily as Joe ended the story by saying plaintively, "So you see, Mr. Mannering, how I get the crow."

"I don't think we need worry about precedence these days," said Grandfather. "Anyway, you are on the list I mentioned. What about the young man? He is allowed to have a hobby."

"I've got a hobby now," said Joe. "I save stamps when I think of it."

"Not that kind of a hobby," said Mr. Mannering. "The hobby is a small falcon from Europe that visits Britain in the summer. There is none out here, although some folk call the Little Falcon the Australian hobby."

Suddenly young David gave a merry laugh, causing Grandfather and Joe to look at him inquiringly.

"It just struck me, Grandfather," said the boy. "Joe's private hunting hawk should be the kestrel and there are plenty of those in Australia."

"Kestrel?" asked Grandfather, puzzled. "Why a kestrel?"

"Table of precedence, you know," grinned David and old Mr. Mannering looked at him sternly.

"You shouldn't criticise your friends like that, David," he said.

"Don't get it. What's all this about?" demanded Joe. "What use would I have for a blessed kestrel?"

"David is trying to be funny," replied Mr. Mannering. "In the table of precedence, as I just told you, the kestrel is reserved for a knave."

"Oh, is it?" snorted Joe. "Remind me to dong you for that."

"I've got a rotten memory," replied David with a grin.

"Anyway," Joe went on, after poking a face at his friend. .. this falconry business is very interesting. Pity they don't go in for it these days. It would be fun, I reckon."

"It was considered a very noble and gentle sport centuries ago," remarked Grandfather. "It is still carried on in some parts of the world, but not as a knightly sport, of course. It had quite a vogue in the United States just before the last war. The old Earl of Rockvale was steeped to the gills in falcon history and was never tired of talking about it. If he had had his way, everyone would have been rushing around the countryside with hawks on their fists, hunting birds and making proper pests of themselves.

"As to the sport itself, that of course goes right back into the dim and distant past. According to Rockvale, the Chinese went hawking 4000 years ago. It certainly was the chief sport of the English nobility from Alfred right up to James the First."

"The joker who burned the cakes?" asked Joe.

"Quite so. The joker who burned the cakes," assented Mr. Mannering. "Incidentally, falconry is training the hawks. Hawking is using them in the field for the actual hunting. The old Saxons went hawking before the Norman invasion. When William the Conqueror landed and settled down, he and his knights went in for it in a big way. They imported gyrfalcons by the boatload from Scandinavia. King Henry the Second was absolutely crazy about the sport and so was Richard the First, who hawked in between crusades in the Holy Land. Why, even that slippery customer, King John, relaxed with his falcons when he was not signing Magna Cartas and trying to throw Robin Hood out of Sherwood Forest."

"That's just a lot of hooey," said Joe.

"I beg your pardon," said Grandfather austerely. "It is the truth. King John did go hawking."

"I didn't mean him. I meant that stuff about Robin Hood. He was just fictitious."

"Possibly. I do not know. But we are dealing now with the history of falconry, not outlaws, real or imaginary," said Grandfather severely.

"Beg your pardon," said Joe.

"Granted," said Grandfather.

"Edward the Third thought more of his hawks than his queen ..." he commenced.

"Gosh, here's that joker again!" groaned Joe.

"Don't keep interrupting me," said Grandfather. "As I was saying, when Edward the Third invaded France in the bow and arrow days, he and his son the Black Prince took no less than thirty falconers with them."

"The Aboriginal boy again," muttered Joe.

"They hawked every spare moment they got," said Mr. Mannering. "All the kings of England up to James the First were keen falconers. Even old Queen Bess had a shot at it in between sharing with Sir Francis Drake and Sir Walter Raleigh the pirate spoils those gentlemen collected on the Spanish Main. James the First was so enthusiastic that he used to invite King Louis the Thirteenth of France and teams of French noblemen to go to England for contests with British knights."

"Test matches, huh?" asked Joe.

"Yes," said Grandfather. "Also, it is a historic fact that one of King James's knights, Sir Thomas Monson, spent £2000 before he managed to get a cast—that is, a pair—of gyrfalcons which he considered were suitable enough for hawking."

"Was he quite right in the head?" inquired Joe.

"I presume so, why?"

"Two thousand quid in those days would be equal to ten thousand quid now. He must have been clean off his nut."

"Shall we say that he was a little over-enthusiastic?" said Mr. Mannering. "Remember, it was his hobby. People, provided they have the money, will spend vast sums on their hobbies. Look at stamp collectors. They will cheerfully pay £1000 for some rare specimen."

"Stark, staring, raving mad, throwing good dough away like that," said Joe decisively.

"Well, be that as it may, falconry flourished up to the time of the civil war in England. Cromwell and his Roundheads were severe types who looked with disfavor on everything gay and in any case the nobles, or Cavaliers, were too busy saving their heads and dodging Cromwell to go hawking. No, the civil wars saw the end of falconry as a popular and general pastime. If I remember falcon history correctly, the last member of the British Royal Family to indulge in it was Frederick, Prince of Wales and son of

George II. Actually, fashion had a lot to do with it. As soon as the reigning king gave it up, his courtiers did likewise."

"Maybe we could start a new fashion out here in Australia," said Joe with a thoughtful frown. "We have plenty of hawks and plenty of wide open spaces."

"I am afraid that falconry will never take on again anywhere," said Grandfather. "Of course quite a number of enthusiasts in various countries indulge in it to this very day as a sort of personal pastime, but as a popular sport, never again. As to hawks, there are at least twenty-four different species in Australia. Most of them could be trained for hawking if a person had the time and the patience to do it."

Old Mr. Mannering paused and there was a faraway look in his eyes. His thoughts were reaching back over the centuries to those romantic days when every gallant knight and his fair lady fared forth into the fields and the forests with hawk on wrist. . . .

Presently he sighed gently and smiled faintly.

"Scoff as you might at the enthusiasm displayed by the ancient falconers, you must admit, lads, that a sport that could get such a grip on the world must have had its particular fascination. It is years since I have given more than a passing thought to it, but now that you two have brought it back to mind, I must confess that I should like to see a revival of it.

"Think of it," he went on, more to himself now than to the boys, "picture to yourselves the ancient sport of kings! Horse-racing is supposed to be that sport now, but how can it possibly take the place of the noble art of falconry?"

"Dunno," said Joe, who felt called upon to say something. But Grandfather did not hear him.

"You've read about Marco Polo and his famous trips to the East, haven't you? Well, if you can believe all he wrote, and he seems to have been a truthful man, Kublai Khan, the great Emperor of

Tartary and China, went hawking with no less than 10,000 falconers with a vast number of gyrfalcons, peregrine falcons, sakers and vultures. It must have been a stupendous event."

"Suffering snakes!" ejaculated Joe. "I'll bet some of the hawks went short of a feed! How could they all do a bit of good for themselves if 10,000 of them were hunting at the same time?"

"I doubt if they sent up the whole lot at once, Joe," laughed the old man. "It must have cost Kublai Khan a few pounds to keep all the falconers employed, apart from the hawks. But they did not seem to consider the expense. Back in the eighth century France had a ' grand fauconnier' who looked after the State's 300 hawks. He was a most important official and was paid 4000 florins a year. That would be £200 in today's money—small enough now but an enormous sum in those remote days.

"And the trouble they went to! There are stories out of India of large hawks being trained to hunt the antelope, wild boar, gazelle and stag. The birds dropped on the animal's head and picked his eyes out!"

"Hey, break it down, Mr. Manneringl" said Joe with a shudder. "That's crook."

Grandfather smiled but did not comment.

"A little while ago I mentioned Magna Carta..." he commenced.

"Yeah," grunted Joe, "signed by King John at Runnymede on June 15, 1215."

"Eh?" exclaimed Grandfather in astonishment. "How did you know that?"

"Seeing that it is the sort of tripe they belt into us at school, no wonder I know it," snorted Joe. "I can recite all the kings and queens of England from William the Conqueror to Queen Elizabeth II. Fat lot of good it does me, but I had to learn it."

"Yes. But about Magna Carta," said the old man. "There is a part of it called 'Carta de Foresta' or the Charter of the Forest which the barons made King John sign and which is, of course, quite obsolete now. But under it, all free men were allowed to go hawking. Before that, only the high and mighty were permitted, as I told you before."

"Yes," said Joe.

"But Edward the Third put his foot down on that a little," said Grandfather.

"Yes, he would! My old mate!" grunted Joe. "What did he do to spoil things?"

"He didn't spoil things exactly, but he made a stringent law ordering every person who found a hawk of any species to take it to the sheriff of the county, or do two years in the nearest dungeon. The theft of a hawk was regarded as an awful crime. The offender, if he did not lose his head, did not see his family for ever so long. In the days of Henry VII, the penalty for stealing or destroying a falcon's egg was a year and a day in the dungeons. Queen Elizabeth I reduced it to three months, even though she was a most enthusiastic falconer herself.

"H'm, yes, it is a great pity in a way that the sport has died out," he concluded.

"The sport, yes, but not the penalties," said Joe. "Gosh, they were a tough lot of coots in those days."

"Yes."

"But all the same," said Joe practically, "that doesn't get us any closer to the actually training of the hawks, does it, huh?"

CHAPTER FOUR

The Falconer's Art

"THE art of the falconer," said Grandfather Mannering to his two small but intensely-interested listeners, "is one wat requires not only the greatest skill, but the greatest patience, coupled with a knowledge of the ways and lives of the birds and a real love of them."

"I'd be willing to give it a go," said Joe, and the old man could not help smiling at his eagerness.

"Take my advice and forget it," said Mr. Mannering. "It takes weeks to train a hawk to hunt. It is a tedious job—much more difficult and complicated than training a racehorse or even a squad of performing fleas."

"I'd still be willing to give it a go," responded Joe with boyish determination.

"Me too," supplemented his friend David.

"Maybe Mr. Mannering would help us," said Joe diffidently but hopefully.

"Well, Joe, I don't know about that. It is many years since I had anything to do with training falcons. Now if it were my old dad, he'd jump in and help you straight away. In fact, he'd do the job for you."

"But you know how to do it, don't you, Mr. Mannering?"

"Oh, yes. I had more than a hand in it in my younger days. I haven't forgotten the art by any means; but as I said before, you had better forget the matter. It would take up too much of your time and in any case you've first got to find your falcon."

"Oh, we'll get one, never fear about that!" said the confident

Joe. "This is the breeding season for all birds, you know."

"I know that. In any case, it is not absolutely necessary to get a young one to train. A fully-grown falcon can be trained just as easily. But it has to be a female bird, not a tiercel."

"Third bird out of the googy," said Joe. "Could you tell us something about how to go about training one? I think we could get a young one out of a nest easier than trying to catch an old one."

"Oh, I'll tell you how it is done and I'll tell you in bitter detail, too. And I'll wager that before I'm half-way through my lecture you'll beg me to stop and you will give up the idea," said Grandfather grimly.

"You can't scare us, Mr. Mannering," said Joe stoutly. "You'll see!"

"Very well then," said the old man briskly. "Here we go. And pay attention without interrupting. We will start off from the point where we have caught our eyas."

"But aren't we going to train a falcon?" said Joe gropingly.

"If you are going to learn falconry, you are going to learn the correct terms, too—terms that have been used for centuries," said Grandfather severely. "An eyas is a young bird in the nest."

"Go on!" said Joe.

"I will. And when a falcon flies in circles above your head, she is said to 'wait on.' She 'stoops' when swooping with closed wings from a height on to her prey and 'binds' when she grabs it in the air and comes down with it. If she soars high above the prey she is said 'to tower.' Should she seize her prey in the air and fly away with it, she 'carries.' Your falcon 'rakes off' when she flies straight away without soaring, and 'checks' when she changes the bird in pursuit."

"Go on!" repeated Joe, but feebly.

"Sure you want me to go on? Still want to train hawks?" asked Grandfather.

"Yes, because, after all, we don't have to use all that silly twaddle, do we?"

"It is not silly twaddle!" snorted the old man. "It is highly dignified, technical falconry language. But, as you say, a hawk can be trained without it. Very well. Now we come to the actual training details. First of all, you must not take a young bird from the nest until its feathers have replaced the down. Birds taken too young are not worth anything."

"Why not?" Joe wanted to know.

"Because they are not, and don't interrupt me," said Mr. Mannering testily. "When you get your eyas you erect a platform in a shed and cover it with straw. This platform has got to be so high that you can just reach it to feed the bird. And that has to be done three times a day—on fresh, lean beef—and kept up while she is growing. As soon as she is strong enough and able to fly, strong, thin, leather straps about six inches long are placed around her legs. These straps are called jesses and they remain on the bird's legs permanently. They are used to tie her to your wrist or to the feeding platform. Then of course you must have a lure. Most essential."

"And what might this lure arrangement be?" asked Joe.

"It is a most important gadget. It is what brings the falcon back to you after she has made an unsuccessful flight. When she is being trained she is fed from it every day. The one my old dad used was made out of a couple of pigeon's wings tied together on a flat round lump of lead covered with leather on which a hunk of raw meat was tied on both sides."

"Where did he get the pigeon's wings from?" asked David.

"Off a dead pigeon, of course. Where else?" grunted Grandfather. "Anyway, a bunch of feathers will do almost as well."

"And easier to get, too," put in Joe.

"Yes. But where did I get when you side-tracked me? Oh, yes. We got as far as the eyas being able to fly. Well then, she is now allowed partial liberty—you let her fly about a bit on her own—which is called 'flying at hack.' It is done so that the hawk will gain strength of wing. You have to be very punctual about feeding her, too, giving her at first good fresh beef finely chopped up with a new-laid egg mixed with it, every second day. Later you can give her freshly killed birds and rabbits."

"Oh, can I?" murmured Joe.

"You not only can, but must," said Mr. Mannering. "Didn't I tell you that training falcons was a long and involved business?"

"Yes, and I'm beginning to think so, too," said Joe, scratching his head. "Anyway, let's hear the rest of it."

"Right. Actually, I haven't started on it yet. The hard part is still to come."

"Oh, my gosh," groaned Joe.

"Quite so. You have to put a hood on the bird. This hood is made of soft leather to fit her and to block out the light, with one hole in it for her beak to stick out of. There is a slit at the back with laces to tie it on. The idea of blindfolding her is to make sure that she sits perfectly still and doesn't flutter and break her feathers as she might do if scared by strangers. She has to get used to them. The best place to practise putting on the hood is in a darkened room. While she has the hood on, you feed her by laying meat across her feet for her to pull at. Later, when she will feed well by candlelight with the hood off, and then by daylight, she may be fed by hand in the open air with people around her."

"How about coming out shooting birds with our catapults?" suggested David.

"Stay where you are," said Grandfather sternly. "You asked for it and you're going to get it if I have to nail the pair of you down. I can't see you two training any falcons. You are too impatient. And patience is a virtue in this game. Which brings me to the next step.

"When training your falcon, you must take her on your wrist two or three hours at a time and stroke her gently. You have got to treat her with the utmost tenderness and consideration and remember always to feed her from the hand. When she has sufficient confidence to spring to the hand for food and has been well broken into the hood, she should be practised at the lure and then flown at a wild bird."

"Stone the blessed crows!" muttered Joe.

"Stone 'em by all means, if you like, but they are no good for hunting. Waste of time. But I admit they make good prey for a falcon. But to get on with it. You've got to train the eyas to come to the lure to be fed. When she is tame enough to sit on a perch in the open air, you should feed her from your gloved hand. Bit by bit you increase the distance from the perch until she has to fly to your hand to get a feed. Now comes a very vital part of the work."

"What is that?" asked David, who was deeply interested.

"She is called off to the lure. This means that you tie a long length of string to the jesses—the leather straps on her legs that I told you about—and then put the hood on her while she is sitting on the wrist of one of your mates. You stand off about thirty yards and swing the lure about. Your mate takes off the hood and the bird will fly to the lure to get a feed."

"Yes, but supposing she doesn't? A bloke would look a fool," said Joe. "She can't get away, anyhow. That is why the long line is tied to her feet. Practice will do the trick. She will learn to fly from your mate's hand to the lure, make no mistake about that. And when she gets there you must reward her with a bit of the meat from the lure. You have to keep this up for days and days and days until she can be trusted to fly without a line on her leg. When you are satisfied that she is doing all right, you next let her have a go at a live bird on the end of a long string. Let her fly off the wrist and kill this bird. Practise this a few times and then you can enter her at the quarry."

"Do what? Take her down into the quarry? What for?" Joe asked, a little bewildered.

"Entering her at the quarry means, in falconry, letting her go at wild birds in the field," said Grandfather.

"Okay," said Joe, heaving a weary sigh. "What comes next?"

"Nothing. That's about all there is to it," said Mr. Mannering.

"About all. Not much, huh?" said Joe, a little sarcastically. "Seems to me a man would have to spend the best years of his life at this mug's game."

"Didn't I tell you all that at first? So you've changed your mind about it, eh?"

"No fear. I'll give it a go. If some knight in a tin suit could do it centuries ago, why can't I?"

"The knights did not do it themselves. They employed experienced falconers."

"Leave it to Sir Joseph McKenzie," said David with a grin.

"And that's just the man to do it," said Joe confidently. He paused. "That is, of course, if Mr. Mannering will lend a hand."

"I might at that," said Grandfather. "As a matter of fact, I wouldn't mind it at all. But first we have to catch our eyas."

"Leave that to me, Mr. Mannering," said Joe with a confidence he did not feel. Joe did not even know if there was a falcon's nest within a thousand miles of where he stood. He was not even sure that he would know a falcon if he stubbed his toe on one. He was, however, a sunny optimist by nature and felt certain that if he put his mind to it he could find possibly a dozen nests each filled to overflowing with eyasses.

Old Mr. Mannering, who was a shrewd man, guessed what was passing in the boy's mind and, with a twinkle in his eye, put a direct question: "Would you know a peregrine falcon if you saw one?"

"Sure thing!" said Joe promptly.

"What does one look like then?"

"Well it is a bird with a hooked beak and claws, and, er, feathers ..." began Joe lamely.

"Never mind, Joe," laughed the old man. "As I told you, I've seen them around these parts. Over in O'Brien's paddock, as a matter of fact. I'll identify one for you later.

"Hard birds to understand, are hawks," he went on thoughtfully. "I've seen 'em flying over the fields where there are plenty of birds that they could grab easily, and seen them make a dive at a rabbit or something else and most likely miss it. I've seen lots of little birds band together and plague the life out of a hawk. He could have killed half a dozen of them if he wanted to, but he just ignored them. Sometimes a hawk will snatch a bird or a mouse and carry it for a long way before dropping it deliberately. It cannot be because of hunger. He just grabs the creature because it is his nature.

"But they are great fliers, though, those hawks. I've seen 'em, and especially the little kestrels, hovering in one place for minutes on end when there hasn't been a breath of wind to help them. Of course, they do not need a breeze to keep them up, like some birds. The peregrines never hover, however. They always soar and circle."

"Did you ever catch any full-grown hawks in England, Mr. Mannering?" inquired Joe.

"Quite a few. It wasn't very difficult. You see, hawks have a habit of perching on the top of dead trees and bare poles, much the same as the crows. They like a clear space where they can look in all directions for their prey. We used to put snares on top of the bare trees and posts and catch them that way."

"What for, to train in falconry?"

"No, to kill them. They were very destructive. They killed off the partridges and pheasants and other game birds which we reared for shooting."

"But didn't you say that you used to train some falcons for the Earl of Rockvale to hawk with?"

"One or two. They were always eyasses out of a nest. The old earl used to go out with his friends and set the falcons on to such things as cranes, magpies, rooks and ravens. He did his partridge, grouse and pheasant hunting with guns. And many a time he would shoot down wild hawks he saw in the trees. They did great destruction among the young game birds in the early summer and also cleaned up the rabbits. Of course hawks do not do as much damage as the weasels and stoats, possibly because they are fewer, but they do enough."

"Never heard of them," said Joe.

"There are no weasels in Australia, or stoats either, but there are plenty of them in New Zealand. They were introduced years ago in the hope that they would kill off the rabbits, which are almost as big a pest there as they are in Australia. It hasn't done much good for New Zealand, though. I suppose it is because the rabbits breed too fast for them. It is different in England where rabbits are slower breeding. From what I hear and read, weasels and stoats are utter pests in New Zealand, killing more poultry than rabbits."

"They ought to go in for myxomatosis over there the same as us here in Aussie," said Joe. "That stuff fixes them goodoh."

"Have you ever seen a rabbit under the influence of myxomatosis, Joe?" asked Mr. Mannering gravely, and when the boy shook his head, the old man said quietly, "Let us hope that you never do. Rabbits are useless pests as we all admit, but..." He shook his head and refused to pursue the subject.

"What do these weasels look like, anyway?" Joe wanted to know.

"Well, the nearest you have to them in Australia is the ferret. I suppose you know what a ferret is?"

"Oh, yes. They use 'em for getting rabbits out of burrows. My father once had one. Sneaky, ugly looking coots of things," said Joe.

"Well, the weasel belongs to the same family, but he is a tough animal and sudden death to small birds and animals. He looks something like a ferret but is different in color. You know what a ferret looks like-pale yellow or white with red eyes. The weasel is mostly reddish brown with white or yellowish underparts and a black-tipped tail. Some of the northern European weasels turn white in winter.

"But you should see a weasel after a rabbit!" said Mr. Mannering.

"I've heard stories of your Australian dingo and tiger cat and all the rest of them, but they are not a patch on the weasel. Once he starts to hunt a rabbit he never stops until he gets it. And he never changes his mind. I mean, if he is after a particular rabbit, he sticks to it, no matter if a dozen others cross his path.

"He looks a bit like a snake, does the weasel, with his long neck and body and stumpy legs. When he picks on a certain rabbit, the chase is on. The rabbit can go in and out of burrows, drainpipes, through hedges, ditches, bushes, more burrows and holes and the weasel follows him. He will even push another rabbit out of the way to get at the one he is after. The other rabbits never help their unfortunate brother, either. I've seen a rabbit hunted by a weasel go into a burrow and get tossed out by those already in there. They don't want any trouble with a weasel.

"The hunted rabbit has no chance at all, for where he can go, the weasel can follow. At last the rabbit is completely exhausted and becomes an easy kill for his enemy. Sometimes weasels hunt in packs. Stoats are something like weasels, but bigger and stronger and tougher."

"That's very interesting, Mr. Mannering. But getting back to training falcons. What are we going to do about that?" asked Joe.

"What do you want to do?"

"Why, give it a go. Catch one and train it," said Joe simply. Old Mr. Mannering laughed. "Go ahead," he invited. "I'll tell you what: you catch a falcon and I'll help you train it. That's a promise." "Gee, Mr. Mannering, good on you," said the grateful Joe. "But, er, where will I find one?"

"I've noticed four of them in O'Brien's paddock," said the old man. "They are two old birds and two eyasses. I've often seen them there. It must be their favourite hunting ground. If you like, we will stroll over there some time and I'll point them out to you, seeing that you apparently would not know a peregrine falcon if one stopped you in the street and said good day to you."

"Okay, let's get a move on," said Joe briskly, not the least offended by Grandfather's remark.

"Here, not so fast, young man," protested Mr. Mannering. "I've had my daily walk in the bush today. Tomorrow morning will be time enough."

"Aw, gee, they might fly away or something might kill them all before then," said Joe.

"That will be just too bad, then," said Grandfather.

Joe was disappointed, but he had to accept Grandfather's edict. He told the old man that he would be on tap next morning bright and early. "Me too," said David enthusiastically.

CHAPTER FIVE

Another Kind of Hunter

THE following morning found Joe, true to his threat, on the Burton doorstep before the family had finished breakfast, and he was forced to kick his heels in idleness until Grandfather and David had got through their bacon and eggs.

It was a very warm and sultry morning, atmospheric conditions welcomed by those lovers of the sun, the cicada tribe. The hotter the day, the better those noisy insects liked it, and as Joe mooned around the Burton backyard, the cicada orchestra struck up in full force its ear-deafening din.

"Noisy coots of things, those locusts," grunted Joe, wandering across to a tree from which came a wave of sound. He gave the trunk a few shakes without subduing the orchestra and then decided to collect a "double-drummer" so that it could give a personal performance. He was about to shin up the tree when old Mr. Mannering emerged from the house, followed by David.

"Have a rest till I collect a double-drummer," he called out. "We can have music with us as we go along."

"Music, my foot!" said Grandfather inelegantly. "Never mind the cicadas. We don't want to take our own performers along. There are plenty where we are going. Let's get a move on in case the falcons do not stay long in the paddock."

But as Joe was already up the tree and as there were several cicadas within reach, he decided that it was worth while wasting a few seconds to secure his portable musician. Thus, when he joined Mr. Mannering and David, he had with him the best specimen of a double-drummer that could be procured in so short a time.

As they walked along, Joe kept shaking the insect in his closed hand, causing it to produce a shrill noise that made Grandfather's head throb.

"Look, chuck that thing away, for goodness' sake, Joe," he exclaimed. "It's bad enough that they are all around us in the trees and bushes, without us having one right up against our earholes. Go on, throw it away, I tell you."

Joe darted a rebellious glance at the old man, but did as he was told. He did not want to run the risk of Grandfather cancelling the falcon expedition. The released cicada circled in wobbly flight before making for the nearest bush, there to add its quota to the din.

"Interesting things, cicadas," said Grandfather as they made their way towards O'Brien's paddock. "They spend most of their lives underground."

"What for?" asked Joe.

"Because it is their nature to do so," said Mr. Mannering. "From the time the mother cicada lays her eggs in the trees until the hatched young ones grow to adult size and lay their own eggs, six or up to eight years have gone by. The American cicada spends no less than seventeen years under the ground."

"Doing what?" demanded Joe.

"Eating and growing," said Grandfather.

"Sounds daft to me," said Joe.

"Haven't you ever seen cicadas coming out of the ground and climbing tree trunks, where they split their skins, dry their wings, and reach maturity?"

"Yes, I've seen all that," replied Joe. "When they come out of the ground they look like little crayfish. Ugly little coots they are."

"They are like that from the day they are hatched. The mother cicada lays her eggs in the bark of trees and when the young ones come out, they are about the size of a flea and are yellow-coloured. Then they drop to the ground and dig into the earth."

"Drop to the ground?" asked David. "Don't they break their silly necks?"

"Not at all. No matter how high the tree is, they don't get hurt. Their bodies are very light. But as soon as they reach the ground they burrow into it, keeping to the tree roots. They go down long distances, but never leave the roots, because they feed on the sap. They stay below for years and years until they are fully grown, and then they burrow upwards until they reach the open air."

"How is it the ground doesn't fall in on them?" asked David.

"Scientists have proved that they use the tree sap in their bodies to plaster the walls of the burrow," said Grandfather. "It has been noticed, too, that when it reaches the open air, the young cicada, or nymph as it is known at that stage, will not emerge if doesn't like the conditions. It might be a rainy day, or it might be too hot. Generally, the nymph waits until evening before coming out, but not always. Anyway, when it does emerge, it makes its way to the nearest tree or upright object, scales it and finds a suitable spot to dig its claws into.

"And it certainly possesses decent claws. They are large and sharp. They have to be, to enable the nymph to dig its way out of the ground in the first place. The insect is also covered from head to tail in a tough skin. This splits down the back, and in due course the adult cicada comes out. You've seen it of course, plenty of times—the soft body and the crumpled wings. However, these soon dry and expand and in next to no time the cicada flies off to add its noise to the others—that is, of course, if it happens to be a male insect. The females do not have the drums to make a row."

"The locusts make the row by rubbing their hind legs across the drums," remarked Joe knowingly.

"That is just where you are wrong, and in any case they are not locusts," said Grandfather. "They don't rub their legs across the drums at all. It is all done by vibration. Underneath the drums on each side of the cicada's body is a hole covered with skin and full of muscles. The insect, using these muscles, causes the skin to vibrate in and out and the drum acts as a sort of amplifier or loud-speaker. The faster the cicada vibrates his muscles, the louder and harsher is the row he kicks up."

"But why the heck does he do it, anyway?" asked Joe.

"Why do birds sing songs? Why do you hum tunes and whistle them? Even a cicada must have his pastime," said Grandfather. "It is said, however, that the row is his love song to the female cicadas. All girls, even human ones, like music."

"All I can say is that the cicada girls must be easily satisfied," said David with conviction.

"They do say that love is blind, you know," laughed Mr. Mannering. "And stone-deaf where the cicada sheilas are concerned," said Joe with a grin.

The three falcon searchers were passing a sandy patch of ground which lay at the side of the bush track along which they were making their way, when David's attention was drawn to the antics of a large, handsome, long-legged insect. It was running around in circles, pushing pebbles aside, thrusting its head under dead leaves and generally acting as if it had something on its mind. David stopped and pointed it out to his companions.

"Looks like a Scotchman searching for a lost sixpence," Joe commented. "What the heck is it? A dirty big hornet, huh?" He stopped and picked up a stone with the obvious intention of putting a permanent end to the insect's business worries.

"Leave it alone," said Mr. Mannering. "Just wait a moment and you'll see something interesting. That isn't a hornet. It's a giant sand wasp and it is looking for a good place to dig its nesting hole. It lives on your friends the cicadas, or rather, its young ones do. Let's watch it for a minute or two and see what it does."

The sand wasp, a large handsome lady with yellow wings and black and orange body, continued its restless search until at length it found what appeared to be a desirable location for a modern residence. It made a few tentative scratches at the ground with its powerful front legs, and then set to work in real earnest. As the three humans watched interestedly; the wasp dug with great speed, the dirt shooting between her hind legs in a thin stream.

"Just like a fox terrier burying a blessed bone," commented Joe, with admiration in his tones. "Gosh, he can travel, can't he?"

"Yes, but it happens to be a she, not a he," said Grandfather.

In next to no time, half of the wasp's body was out of sight, only her hindquarters, supported by her strong back legs, being visible. A couple of times, the insect backed out of the hole carrying a fair-sized pebble in its jaws. These pebbles were dropped a foot or so away from the hole.

David, who had been inspecting the vicinity of the wasp's new home, pointed to several other holes in the ground. Each was big enough for a mouse to crawl into. Mr. Mannering said that these holes would be the burrows of other wasps: that the sandy patch appeared to be a favorite spot for the insects.

By this time there was no sign of the excavating wasp, but the thin jet of dust was still shooting from the hole she was making. Joe picked up a large pebble and would have dropped it into the burrow on top of the busy insect had not Grandfather restrained him.

"Why can't you leave her alone!" said the old man. "She isn't doing you a scrap of harm. Bless me, but boys can be thoughtless."

"Just wanted to see her kick this rock out," grunted Joe, a little surlily.

"Hey, Grandfather, Joe, have a look at what's coming along here!" exclaimed David. "Gee whizz, you wouldn't read about it!"

Coming down the path at a brisk pace was another sand wasp, and it was transporting, without any trouble, a fullgrown cicada. The cicada was on its back and the wasp was carrying it between its long legs. It held the cicada's body with its front legs and used its middle and hind pairs to get over the ground. Occasionally it bumped into dead twigs and stones, but these did not halt its progress; it just knocked them out of the way.

Reaching the sandy patch, the wasp went quickly across it, passing close to the hole the other wasp was digging, and getting showered with light dust. It made straight for a hole and vanished down it, taking the cicada with it.

"Now what?" asked Joe. "Will the wasp settle down and have a feed underground?"

"No, she will not," said Grandfather. "I told you before that the adult wasp doesn't eat cicadas. She stores them up for her young ones."

"How?" David wanted to know.

Mr. Mannering explained that the sand wasp dug a burrow about two or three feet in length and made shorter tunnels from the main one. At the end of these branches it dug a round chamber large enough to store a cicada. To catch one of these noisy insects, the wasp jumped on its back when it wasn't looking, and stung it. The sting contained a fluid which caused instant paralysis and the cicada fell to the ground insensible, but not dead. The wasp then transported it to its burrow and as soon as each chamber contained a cicada, the wasp laid an egg on each inert body. The cicada stayed alive for some days and provided succulent food for the young wasp grub hatched out. The grub invariably reached maturity before the cicada-food had given out, and then it spun itself into a cocoon like many other grubs. In due course it emerged as a black and orange sand wasp, ready to take up its own cicada-killing duties.

"That is, of course, if it is a lady wasp," said Grandfather. "The males are not interested in cicadas. All they seem to do is loaf around with other males and just feed their faces."

"Do they eat cicadas?" asked David.

"No; only wasps in the grub stages do that. The adult wasps live on honey from flowers and sweet sap from trees. Which reminds me of the fact that some of them have even been known to drag cicadas away from holes they have made in the bark of a tree and suck up the sap themselves."

"You mean that the wasps, as well as taking the cicadas home to feed their young ones on, actually pinch the sap from the cicadas for themselves, after the cicadas have had to bore a hole in the tree to get it?" exclaimed Joe.

"Exactly. I've seen them at it," said Mr. Mannering.

"Rubbing it in a bit, isn't it?" exclaimed David.

"No doubt about that. It seems to be a habit with all wasps, this business of adding insult to injury. There was an American scientist visiting Rockvale Manor years ago while I was there. He was interested in falconry and was picking up details for a book he was writing. In talking about hawks, he mentioned that in South America there is a wasp that acts like a hawk, but her prey is the tarantula spider.

"This wasp, a fierce big brute of a steel-blue colour, is known as the Tarantula Hawk and the female's only prey is the spider of that name, which itself is huge and very fierce. Quite a different proposition compared with this sand wasp of ours which kills harmless cicadas. The tarantula spider fights back and is quite capable of killing the wasp; but it rarely succeeds.

"Anyway, this American scientist said that the tarantula hawk hunts the tarantula spiders like a falcon hunts other birds. When it sights a spider it hovers over it until it gets the chance to strike and then does so like lightning. One sting and the spider is paralysed. If the wasp should miss the first time, it alights on the ground and then there is a free-for-all fight, the wasp winning nine times out of ten.

"But I mentioned earlier that it seemed to be a habit of wasps to add insult to injury. These tarantula hawk wasps aim to locate a spider that is near its home, which is usually a burrow in the earth. Having found one, the wasp drops to earth, getting between the spider and its tunnel. In the ensuing fight the odds are on the wasp. Having put the spider out of action, she calmly drags it down its own burrow, lays an egg on it, seals up the hole and goes about her businesswhich is looking for another tarantula spider to treat likewise."

"Well, what do you know about that for cheek!" breathed David. "The spider's home becomes its tomb."

"Ain't nature wonderful!" murmured Joe, apropos of nothing.

Leaving the wasps to their own devices, the three falcon hunters proceeded on their way, and in due course reached O'Brien's paddock.

CHAPTER SIX

"Operation Blue Wren"

BLISSFULLY unaware of the plans being formulated by certain human beings to revive the ancient sport of falconry with a member of her family as the star performer of the revival, Black-cheek, perched on the summit of the dead tree in O'Brien's paddock, had her own irritating problem to solve. It was a problem that should never have arisen.

It was futile, frivolous, unnecessary and actually unworthy of such a bird as Black-cheek, the imperious and formidable peregrine falcon. She was cross and unhappy because she was unable to catch a small blue wren. Why she should worry at all over this dainty little fairy-like creature which would hardly make one solid mouthful as a feed, when there were many other birds, together with rabbits and other satisfying food for the taking, was a matter that Tiercel and her two young eyasses could not understand. But there it was.

In the paddock was a dense patch of scrub and thickets and in this tangled undergrowth there dwelt a family of fairy blue wrens headed by Blue Cap. None of them ever ventured into the open field and it was that annoying fact that irritated Black-cheek. The little birds kept close to their thicket where there was plenty of insects for them. On several occasions the falcon had dived at Blue Cap, but the dainty little fellow with his jaunty cocked-up tail had always been too quick for her. He spent more time on the ground at the edge of the scrub than perched on the local twigs and the speed with which he could dive into the impenetrable thickets baffled Black-cheek and made her despair ever of catching him.

Blue Cap's nest was a dome-shaped structure with a side entrance protected by a hood. It was made of grass, cobwebs and bark fibre and warmly lined inside with feathers, hair and wool. It was placed in a tuft of grass which grew in the thickest part of the scrub and it contained three reddish-white spotted eggs.

Blue Cap and his mate had used the same nesting place for several seasons and had always managed to rear a family, sometimes two and even three in the one year. Blue Cap was now four years old and, consequently, had his permanent adult plumage.

Black-cheek had often noticed that Blue Cap's wren companions were half a dozen plain brown birds. If she thought about that interesting fact at all, probably she would have wondered if the little blue wren was running a harem with a flock of little brown wives to keep him company.

But Blue Cap had only the one wife. The others were their children. Unlike nearly every other species of bird in the bush, the fairy wren was the complete family man. To call him a bigamist with a flock of wives was to slander him. The general law of the bird world was that as soon as the young ones could take care of themselves, they were turned loose to make their own life plans, leaving their parents free to raise another brood. Youngsters were not encouraged to loaf around the parent nest; in fact, quite a number of them definitely were discouraged by parental beak and claw. In any case, the parents just stopped feeding them and they had to get their own meals or starve.

Not so, however, with the little fairy wrens. As soon as the young ones were old enough to look after themselves, their parents again nested. The fully-grown young ones, instead of leaving home voluntarily or being thrown out neck and crop, stayed on and assisted their parents to care for and feed the new batch. They eventually left to find their own mates, the females first, but as long as they were needed, the young males stayed on to help mum and dad. At the end of the breeding season they took themselves off, leaving their parents with the last of the tribe for that year.

But never at any time were Mr. and Mrs. Blue Cap without the aid of some of their youngsters.

And because all the young birds, male and female, were brown for several seasons, Blue Cap and his gentlemen friends gained the unwarranted reputation of being nothing but a mob of much-married men.

Though he did assist in building the nest and though he was much devoted to his growing family, Blue Cap did not consider it any part of his duty to assist in incubating the eggs. That job belonged wholly to his little brown mate; but during the fourteen days she remained brooding and the subsequent ten or twelve days before the hatched-out young ones left the nest, she had plenty of hands, or rather, beaks, to feed her and the brood.

Blue Cap's sons were not as pretty as he was when they first reached adulthood. The lads resembled their mother in coloring for some time. Then, like a boy emerging from rompers into pants, each developed a dark blue tail and a dark brown bill. Next came black feathers on his neck and chest and the blue cap on top of his head, his cheeks and his back. And very nice, too. But at the end of the breeding season he went and moulted all his beauty and emerged again with a plain brown suit. This happened for three seasons, but at the end of the fourth he was Blue Cap permanently.

Blue Cap might be the prettiest little creature in O'Brien's paddock, but it was a beauty upon which Black-cheek looked sourly. To the falcon, the small wren was merely a meal. And yet he would hardly make one very light snack for such a bird as the predatory hawk. Black-cheek must have realised this, for she was a highly intelligent bird. But in her pig-headed fashion she went to endless and fruitless trouble trying to trap the dainty little will-o'-the-wisp. Perhaps it was wounded pride that would not let her give the game up. For, after all, Black-cheek was one of the fleetest birds in the land. She could chase and catch the swift little green parakeets as they flashed among the twigs and leaves of the trees. Very few birds could do that. And yet she could not catch one small blue wren, a puny little creature that could not even fly very efficiently. Blue Cap could certainly whizz along the ground and dart like lightning into dense thickets out of which no bird could eject him; but he couldn't or wouldn't come right out into the open and give an annoyed peregrine falcon a chance to get him. Once Black-cheek caught Blue Cap away from his thicket, it would be the end of the wren.

Being a tiny bird with no thinking powers, Blue Cap, of course, was unaware of the fact that Black-cheek had specially marked him down as afternoon or morning tea. All he knew was what he had actually experienced—he had been dived at on several occasions by a large bird, but always had managed to elude his enemy because he did not stray away from his chosen patch of scrub into which he could vanish in a split second.

And then one morning Blue Cap was confronted by a menace that he did know and appreciate—a pair of bronze cuckoos. It was age-old instinct that made the wren and his family deeply resent the presence of a cuckoo.

But though there was a pair of these parasites in the neighbourhood, Blue Cap and his friends saw only one at a time. That was part of the cuckoo strategy and cunning—a plan of action evolved by the first cuckoos put on earth when all the world was young.

It was only in the springtime that Blue Cap and his relations and in fact all the other species of small birds upon whom the cuckoos foisted themselves and their eggs—saw these handsome, lazy birds. In the off-seasons they seemed to vanish as it they had never been. But as soon as the first warm days of spring arrived, urging all those birds who were honest enough and industrious enough to build nests to get a move on, up showed the cuckoos like so many poor relations looking for free board and lodging.

And what cunning, knowledgeable birds they were, those

foisterers of eggs upon foster-parents! They knew every move in the game and made very few false steps. So it was with the pair that had designs upon the nest of Black-cheek's pet headache, Blue Cap.

The cuckoos knew just where the wrens' nest was and they knew exactly when to act. Their idea in allowing Blue Cap to see only one of them at a time was designed to hoodwink the little bird. If he thought there was only one of them, and he managed to keep it under observation all the time, he would know if it laid an egg in his nest. The cuckoo plan was that the female should carry out a sneak raid on the wren's nest and deposit her egg while Blue Cap and company were occupied keeping an eye on her mate. Oh, it was a cunning scheme, a scheme that had been carried out with great success by cuckoos right through the ages and in every country in which cuckoos lived.

But the sagacity and cunning of the parasites did not end there. The female knew, or her age-old instinct told her, that if she deposited her egg in Blue Cap's nest too soon, the wrens would desert it. She also knew that if she left it too late and the legitimate eggs were hatched first, her own egg would not fulfil its destiny and produce a chick. The wren's own clutch would not be more than four. When the fourth was laid, that would be the time to act. Common bird procedure was not to start incubating the eggs until the whole clutch had been laid so that all would be hatched out together.

And so the cuckoos waited patiently. As soon as the fourth egg was laid by the wrens, the female cuckoo would lay her own egg on the ground, carry it in her beak to the wren's nest, drop it in and steal a wren's egg to make room for it.

It was another proof of ancient cuckoo cunning that the birds always placed their eggs in the nests of others who ate insects. Should they be foolish enough to select the home of a seed-eater the nestling cuckoo would starve to death. They also were wise enough to pick on a nest which contained eggs of a color somewhat similar to their own.

It must not be supposed that the arrival of the cuckoos in the neighbourhood had been regarded benevolently by the wrens and the other small nest-building residents of O'Brien's paddock. To the contrary.

The first to sight the newcomers was Willy Wagtail, who had a nest in a tree near the paddock waterhole. Willy told every other bird about it in language that was deplorable and attacked the male cuckoo with a viciousness that was also deplorable.

The first appearance of a cuckoo near Blue Cap's nest threw the wren tribe into a panic. Blue Cap, though a tiny fellow, was not a coward and he attacked the cuckoo with everything he had—which wasn't much. The cuckoo took no notice of him at all, but just sat in a low bush and yawned. Then the wren was joined by all his family, Willy Wagtail and his mate, a lark, three honeyeaters and a yellow-tailed thornbill. The scoldings they indulged in and the language they used was quite intimidating, but the cuckoo merely removed himself from the neighbourhood temporarily.

That was the supreme strategy in Operation Blue Wren. The female cuckoo never exposed herself to these attacks. She was awaiting her chance in a secluded spot while her mate took all the abuse and insults. But everything comes to an end at last. The final wren egg was due to be laid on the morrow...

It was a good thing for Blue Cap that during these three or four hectic cuckoo-filled days, Black-cheek was not around, because he certainly could not have eluded her and still assisted in harassing the bronze parasite. It so happened that Black-cheek and Tiercel were visiting the creek for a few days. Their eyasses had now left them, and the falcons were toying with the idea of nesting again.

Blue Cap's mate laid her fourth and last egg to schedule and the two cuckoos knew it. Now was the time to act and have done with it. Mrs. Cuckoo took up her position in a convenient bush not so far away from the wrens' home thicket and kept out of sight. Her mate thereupon flaunted himself in full view of Blue Cap, who was perched on a twig, his jaunty tail at full mast. The wren twittered indignantly and immediately was joined by the two wagtails. If there was going to be any excitement, they were not going to be left out of it. They were itching to have a go at the cuckoo even before Blue Cap's own family could swing into action.

Six little wrens and two wagtails made for the male cuckoo in an undulating flock. The wrens were not such good fliers, but the wagtails were, and they were enjoying themselves immensely. The male cuckoo, which had been perched on an old log in full view of everyone, immediately took to the air and flew into a tree, the wrens and wagtails in full cry. That was just what he wanted. Making sure that they were all following him, he then fled away, but not so fast as to outdistance them. He did not want them to give up the chase too soon.

And as he vanished over the paddock followed by his small pursuers, his mate dropped to the ground from the concealment of her bush. Quickly she laid her egg. Then, taking it up gently in her beak, she spread her wings and rose into the air, intending to fly carefully to the thicket, not fifty feet away, in which Blue Cap's domed nest was hidden.

It was certainly bad luck for the cuckoo, after all her scheming, that Blue Cap, now chasing her mate across the paddock, had incurred the unreasonable anger of Blackcheek the falcon.

Egg in bill, she was about half-way across the space separating her hiding place from the wren's thicket, when a harsh scream rent the air. The cuckoo had no chance to take evasive action. With a high-speed dive and a mighty rush of wings, Black-cheek tumbled from the skies and smashed her to earth. It was not Blue Cap, but Black-cheek wasn't worrying about that.

It was a melancholy end to a fine scheme for, as the triumphant falcon proceeded to dine off the luckless cuckoo, a tribe of foraging ants began to dine off her broken egg ....

CHAPTER SEVEN

Comedians of the Creek

A PRETTY little bird perched on a twig of a weeping willow tree that leaned in tired fashion over the bank of the creek, wiped its beak several times on the twig, fluffed out its feathers and fell into a deep but pleasant reverie. This was Pardalote, the diamond bird. He was a small fellow and very gay in his many-coloured and spotted plumage; and at the moment was indeed feeling rather proud of himself. It was not because of his personal beauty, though Nature had been exceedingly generous to him, her lavish colour brush splashing him with grey, red, yellow, orange and black. He was on good terms with the world and with himself because, in the bank of the creek just below him was his nest, and in that nest was his mate, patiently incubating four pure white eggs.

Mr. and Mrs. Pardalote had accomplished quite a feat of engineering in constructing their nest. They had driven a tunnel into the creek bank for a distance of four feet and at the end had hollowed out a chamber in which they had constructed a cosy home of bark, grass, feathers and other material. These were the two birds that Grandfather had seen taking nesting material into the creek bank tunnel.

Pardalote preened a couple of his wing feathers by running each one carefully through his small bill, and then, for no apparent reason, issued a shrill order: "Pick-it-up, pick-it-up." As there was nobody there to "pick it up" and, in any event, nothing special to pick up, he said "wit-e-chu" six times in succession, left the willow twig and flew off down the creek to see what was doing in the bird world.

There was a great deal doing, for the creek was a very popular place. The willows and gums that lined its banks and the reeds and the water plants that edged its surface were favourite nesting places and foraging haunts for all kinds of feathered residents.

Pardalote's progress downstream was noted idly by many. Sitting on a branch that overhung the water was a willy wagtail, a cousin of the ones living near the waterhole in O'Brien's paddock.

And like the O'Brien's paddock pair who could not keep their beaks out of the affairs of Blue Cap the wren, the creek wagtail was an inquisitive little wretch. As he saw Pardalote passing he felt minded to dart out and engage him in battle; but parental responsibilities prevented him. For, close to where he perched arrogantly swinging his long tail from side to side, his little black and white mate sat tight upon her nest of closely-woven fibre and spider webs. She had laid one cream and brown egg and confidently anticipated adding at least another three to it.

Willy was on guard duty and therefore could not spare the time to go chasing around with diamond birds. He therefore contented himself with screeching at Pardalote.

That small bird eventually decided to have a rest in an ancient spotted gum which leaned tiredly over the creek as if it felt like collapsing on to the water's soft bosom and lapsing into eternal sleep. But it had been there in that same position for many long years and, provided an extra strong gale or an extra special flood did not flatten it, was likely to remain there for a great many years yet to come.

Having given his tail feathers a "lick and a promise" preen, Pardalote lifted one wing and peered searchingly under it. He had felt an itch and desired to find the cause of it. Then his attention was diverted from his wing to a clattering noise which came from further downstream. He could not see what was making the row because there was a bend in the creek, but the fact that he did not flee from the tree proved that he knew he had nothing to fear from the noise creator. This was true enough, because Biziura the musk duck was quite a harmless comedian.

As Pardalote watched from his tree, Biziura and his mate came clattering into view like a pair of small paddlewheel steamers. Except when travelling from water to water across country, and then only at night, Biziura did very little flying. Swimming was his long suit except when scared or in sheer high spirits. Then he used his wings as paddles and splashed away with more noise than necessary.

The two musk ducks came to a full stop underneath Pardalote's tree and began to fossick for waterplants and aquatic creatures at the creek's edge. With his spiked tail and stiff leathery pouch under his bill, Biziura was a hardlooking bird citizen. His mate had the stiff tail without the "tobacco pouch."

Having made a very light snack out of some pond snails and water-beetles he managed to find among the reeds, Biziura decided put on an entertainment for his mate, and for any other creatures that might be interested.

From his high branch, Pardalote had a grandstand view of the old male musk duck as he propelled himself to the very middle of the creek. There he remained in deep thought for a second or two. Suddenly he swam in a rapid circle a few times and then, with rapid back-kicks of his strong webbed feet, shot out jets of water on each side of his body. As he did so he let out deep honks, which echoed down the creek. Next he inflated his tobacco pouch by means of the opening beneath his tongue, threw back his head, spread out his tail and spun round and round on the water like a top. Ceasing this, he looked across at his mate as if seeking her approval, but discovered that she had turned her back on him and was fossicking among the reeds. Quite unabashed by her lack of interest, Biziura deflated his pouch, swivelled his head, placed his beak on his tail and spun round in the water in the direction opposite to that in which previously he had whirled.

Then, growing tired of his sport, he joined his mate among the reeds and Pardalote, the free show over, left his tree and flitted back up the creek towards his nest and his patient little mate.

As he flitted past the tree in which Willy Wagtail had his nest, Pardalote was subjected to a stream of insults that were quite unmerited. Willy Wagtail was in good form. Pardalote increased his speed a little. He was not exactly afraid of Willy, but he wanted no trouble with anyone. Willy sensed this and decided to give him some.

Darting into the air, the long-tailed little villain streaked after the diamond bird, caught up with him and snapped at his tail. Pardalote changed into high gear and fled wildly. Willy whizzed after him, headed him and, having, with marked contempt, looped the loop around him, deliberately dived on to his back and pushed him down almost to waterlevel. Then, with a screech of pure egotism, he looped the loop again and flew back to his tree. Coming to rest on the branch near his nest, he swayed gently to and fro, fixed a beady little eye upon his long-suffering mate and, hypocrite that he was, whispered, "Sweet pretty creature." Mrs. Willy shut her eyes and ignored him.

Pardalote streaked up the creek like a jet plane. All he wanted was the safety of his tunnel where no crazy wagtails could get at him.

But the little bird's adventures were not over yet; for as he came in sight of home, something large flashed across in front of him and made him swerve sharply, to seek refuge among the thick leaves of a tree on the bank. Peering fearfully round the edge of a broad leaf, he tried to locate the bird that had scared him—a kookaburra—and saw it sitting on a branch in a high tree on the opposite side of the stream.

The diamond bird was very much afraid of the giant kingfisher and had every cause to be; for Laughing Jack was the terror of all small feathered creatures—a slaughterbird as bad as, if not worse than, the butcher-bird. Jacky had a great, though undeserved, reputation as a snake-killer and fisherman. The number of snakes he killed was few and small, and as for fish, provided they were in shallow water and too slow to get away, he might catch a small one or two. No, Jacky's main occupation was that of a nest raider. He dragged small nestlings to their doom as an easily-won meal and often killed them just for fun.

What a different bird he was to Black-cheek the falcon and Tiercel her mate, who indulged in aerial combat with their enemies and took their captives on the wing. The falcons scorned to kill birds on the ground and as for raiding nests of small songsters for their helpless young, why, that was unthinkable!

Of course, Pardalote did not think such thoughts as these. He was wholly preoccupied with his own personal safety. He knew that no kookaburra could raid his nest in the creek bank.

But as it happened, Pardalote had no cause for alarm on this occasion. Jacky was building his own nest and at the moment was not thinking of dinner. Across the creek from where he sat was another large gum tree and up its trunk fifty feet from earth was a large black lump. This was a termites' or white ants' nest, and Jacky was turning it into a nest for his own brood. As Pardalote watched, the kookaburra launched himself from his limb and flew swiftly across the stream to the termites' nest, his giant, sharp beak straight in front of him like a sword. He did not pull up, but plunged his beak straight into the black lump. Pulling it free, he returned to the other side of the creek, only to repeat the performance. This he would do over and over again until he had excavated a hole in the termites' nest large enough to hollow out a nesting chamber. There his mate would lay her eggs and they would set up house together.

The little diamond bird waited until the kookaburra flew again at the black lump and then darted swiftly up the creek without Jacky seeing him. Reaching his tunnel, he entered it straight away and soon was telling his little mate in bird fashion the adventures he had encountered. And especially the fact that a kookaburra was taking up residence in the neighbourhood. Those were evil tidings for the wee birds.

On top of the bank, but further back in a patch of scrub, there lived another pair of birds to whom the news that a kookaburra was building a nest nearby was also most unwelcome. Satin the bower-bird and his mate had two fledglings in their nest and they did not want them to form a meal for a hungry kookaburra.

Satin was a beautiful bird in his wholly dark blue-black plumage. His mate was of a more sober greenish colour, but, like him, she was an accomplished architect, actor, painter and decorator.

The two birds had built their bower and playground among some bushes near a big hollow log. After having laid down a platform of sticks, they had erected an arched runway more than a foot high. This was composed of slender sticks which bent over and formed a graceful tunnel. In front of this, and around about it, the birds had arranged a variety of playthings and decorative objects, mostly of a blue colour. They were mad on blue, were Satin and his mate, and had even found on a rubbish-tip some old blue-bags from a human washhouse. There were blue flowers, blue glass, blue string, blue feathers, a blue marble and even a blue cigarette packet. For variety, there were numerous cast-off cicada cases, rusty nails, pebbles, bits of tin, some empty snail shells and even some withered lemon skin.

But blue was their favourite colour. Satin himself had dark blue feathers, or, more correctly, rich violet-blue with various shades of purple. Even his eyes were blue, while his whole coat shone with a satiny gleam. He was always on the lookout for treasures to add to his collection and he was continually arranging and rearranging them for better effect. And he was even a house-painter as well as a decorator. He actually brought charcoal to his bower, chewed it up into a paste and, using a bit of bark as a brush, painted the sticks of the inside walls.

Satin and his mate had their nest in the fork of a gum tree nearby. They were not fools enough to build it on the ground where it would be in handy reach of any marauding bird, animal or human. The nest was fifty feet up the tree and was a shallow affair of sticks and twigs lined with dried leaves. It was drab compared with their bower and playground. But drab or not, it held their two nestlings and if Kookaburra found it, it would be hard luck indeed.

It was at this period of crisis in the lives of the small creek birds that Black-cheek and Tiercel came into the picture. It was after their two eyasses had left home that they decided to look over the creek, a decision which had brought relief to Blue Cap the wren in O'Brien's paddock.

From their high vantage point in the heavens, the waterway stretched out before them like a narrow road flanked by trees. Tiercel dropped down to tree level and began to beat slowly along while Black-cheek followed his progress from higher up. She circled slowly, ready to dive upon anything her mate flushed from cover. She could rely upon him to make short work of birds that were flushed but did not rise. Any that flew above the treetops would be her responsibility.

As she traced her hard, slow circles in the skies, Blackcheek saw everything that went on below her. She saw Satin the bowerbird and his mate darting in and out of their playground and knew that no matter how swift she was, she had little hope of trapping either of them in the open. She saw a magpie making a rapid journey across the stream and she saw the two musk ducks feeding in the reeds.

When the magpie got directly beneath her, she tipped over and dived at him, merely in play. Maggie heard her scream and shot skywards, banked and snapped at her viciously. Black-cheek pulled out of her dive and spiralled gracefully to her former position. She had had no evil designs on Maggie, who had now resumed his journey unhurriedly. She had just felt, for a moment, like indulging in a bit of fun.

Down below, Tiercel was having a fruitless hunt. There were no birds in the trees at all, except a few little yellow-tailed thornbills, and he could not be bothered with them.

Then he saw the kookaburra. The big bird was still digging holes in the termites' nest by shooting across the creek in a feathered bayonet charge. Tiercel rose above Jacky and circled. Black-cheek, far above, wondered what her mate was doing. She could not understand why Tiercel should want to tackle the kookaburra. She knew that he could probably beat Jacky in a fight, but who wanted to eat a kookaburra? Perhaps Tiercel wanted to have some fun like she had tried to have with the uncooperative magpie. Good. She would be in it, too.

Black-cheek tipped sideways and fell over in a dive-bombing drop. She and Tiercel approached Jacky from different sides. Tiercel checked, then shot upwards, but Black-cheek dealt Jacky a blow on the back that made him squawk loudly and dislodged several feathers, which floated idly to earth. Jacky wheeled and pecked savagely, but Blackcheek whirled away and up, to join her mate. It was all good, clean fun, if not for Jacky the kookaburra, certainly for the falcons.

For a few minutes the peregrines described wide circles over the creek and then moved away, heading for O'Brien's paddock and, incidentally, arriving just in time for Blackcheek to thwart the bronze cuckoo.

Down below, Satin the bower-bird and his mate were hiding out of sight under a low bush, waiting patiently for the falcons to clear out. And as they waited, something dropped on to the ground in front of them. Satin eyed it inquisitively, but did not move. The two birds stayed under the bush for half an hour and then, deeming that the coast was clear, emerged and inspected the buff-colored object closely. It was not blue, worse luck, but variety was the spice of life, so, picking up the kookaburra's feather, Satin took it and carefully laid it between a piece of withered orange skin and the empty shell of a pond snail.

CHAPTER EIGHT

The Story of the Eel

GRANDFATHER, Joe and David entered O'Brien's paddock a fair distance away from the lone tree that Black-cheek and her mate used as a watch-tower. "We want to get as close as possible to it without the falcons seeing us and then we can observe them," Mr. Mannering had told the boys.

There were plenty of scrub patches as well as groups of trees and the trio dodged from shelter to shelter until they got within a few hundred yards of the old dead tree. Taking up his position behind a huge stringy-bark, Grandfather unshipped a pair of powerful field glasses and trained them on the watch-tower.

"Not there yet, boys," he said, lowering the binoculars.

"Sure you can see all right, Mr. Mannering?" asked Joe. "Better let me have a crack with those glasses. Your eyesight mightn't be as keen as mine."

"Cheeky young pup," snorted Grandfather. "I might be six times your age, but there is nothing wrong with my eyesight. However, if looking will convince you, go ahead."

He handed the glasses to the eager boy after showing him how to adjust them and Joe trained them on the falcons' look-out. A grunt of disappointment told his companions that he was convinced of the absence of Black-cheek and Tiercel. He was about to hand the glasses to their owner when he saw something that made his previous grunt of disappointment turn to an exclamation of delight.

"Two big birds have just lobbed into the tree," he said excitedly. "Blessed if I know where they came from. Can you see them? One is now perched on top of the tree and the other on the branch down below."

"Yes, and I don't need field glasses to see them, like a certain young shaver I know," said Mr. Mannering pointedly. "But there are only two of them. Last time I was over here, about a week or so ago, there were also two eyasses. I suppose they have grown too old to keep with their parents. H'm. I was hoping that if we did carry out our falconry plan, we could catch a youngster."

"But didn't you say that a full-grown bird could be trained?" demanded Joe. "I'm sure you said that."

"So I did. But if a young one is trained it can be taught all the tricks of the trade and apart from that it would be easier to catch than an adult bird."

He pondered the matter for a moment, while Joe continued to stare at the falcons through the binoculars.

"The best thing for us to do would be to try to locate the nest of these two birds and try to get an eyas," said Grandfather. "They will be breeding again any time now. Perhaps they have already laid their eggs. From my knowledge of these hawks I would say that their nest is away over there among the rocks on that cliff."

He pointed to the rocky eminence about two miles away and just visible in the morning haze.

"I've been up there once or twice," he confessed. "It is an ideal nesting place for falcons and eagles. Of course, in my walks, I never had falcons in mind, so I never thought to go looking for their nests. But I'll explore that cliff thoroughly as soon as I can."

"It wouldn't appeal to me, chasing around rocks and cliffs looking for falcons' nests," said Joe. "Why can't we just shove snares all over that tree and catch the old ones? It would save a lot of time."

"But not a lot of trouble. No, we will first try to find the nest. If we can't, then we might think about snares. It would be a mighty tough job scaling that tree to set snares and they would have to be pretty strong ones to hold those beauties."

"I can scale any tree in the bush," boasted Joe.

"You are not going to scale this one," said Grandfather firmly.

They watched Black-cheek and her mate for some time, but neither bird seemed anxious to go hunting. Truth to tell, they had breakfasted well off a couple of rabbits they had caught on their way to the look-out, so were not particularly hungry. Over a week had now passed since their eyasses had left them and already Black-check was toying with the idea of raising another brood. Before leaving the nest that morning she had made a half-hearted start on cleaning it out.

Grandfather, Joe and David debated what they should do. Grandfather said he was going home, because he could be more profitably employed around the Burton home than spying upon a pair of peregrine falcons, no matter how deeply interested he was in bush lore.

"We will all go home," said Joe. "First of all, I'll go over to that tree and fire a rock from my catapult at the falcons. It might make them fly away home and give us a clue where their nest is."

"All right," said Grandfather, "but just you be careful how you fire the stone. Just scare the birds, don't tumble them from their perches."

Joe replied indignantly that if he wanted to drop the falcons he could; on the other hand, if he desired merely to scare them, that, too, was completely within his capabilities. He knew just where every rock fired from his catapult would land. He was, he added immodestly, an expert with the weapon.

"And with your tongue, too," murmured David, a remark Joe treated with the contempt it deserved.

The three of them emerged from their concealment and proceeded in Indian file, Joe in the lead. And as they neared the ancient tree, the boy fitted a stone into the pouch of the catapult. The falcons watched their approach with wary eyes, but did not move. The trio of humans halted under the tree and stared upwards. Tiercel on his branch was the easier target. Black-cheek on her pinnacle was almost invisible, blocked out by the intervening branch.

"Hit the branch near the bird, and do be careful," counselled Grandfather.

"All right, all right!" snorted Joe. "Get off my back and gimme a break, for the love of Mike! How the heck do you expect me to bring off a difficult shot like this when you're all yapping like a lot of old women at a bargain sale?"

These snappish remarks were received in silence. Joe took aim and fired. The stone did not hit the branch, but sang through the startled Tiercel's tail-feathers and, striking the trunk above, ricochetted and whizzed down past the falcon's head with a hum like an irritated hornet. With a sharp scream Tiercel leaped into the air, several tail feathers falling from him as he did so, and, spiralling upwards, circled high over the treetop. Black-cheek recognised the note of alarm in her mate's scream and immediately joined him.

Circling higher and higher, the two peregrines continued to ring the air above the heads of the three adventures for several minutes. Then Tiercel broke off and flew in the direction of the distant township. Black-cheek, having no interest in her mate's ultimate destination, decided to return home and get a move on with nest-cleaning.

Old Mr. Mannering, knowledgeable in the ways of birds, noted that she was flying towards the distant cliffs where his experience told him her nest might be located. He had no interest in the movements of Tiercel. Bringing his field glasses to bear on the departing Black-cheek, he kept her in sight as she made her unhurried way towards the hilly country. The powerful binoculars showed the old man that the falcon was making for a part of the cliffs where a tree jutted out from the sheer rock face. And as he watched, he saw her alight on a branch. She stayed there for a few moments lazily preening her feathers and then dropped down upon what appeared to be a ledge. Presently she disappeared from view.

"I'm game to bet good money that that is where her nest is," Grandfather told the two boys. "It seems to be an ideal place. I

would say with some confidence that there is a crevice in those
rocks and in that crevice is a peregrine falcon's nest."

As he continued to gaze, he saw the falcon emerge from the cliff
face and fly into the tree. He could not see what she was doing, but
she remained in the tree for only a few seconds. Then she returned
to the crevice. Presently she appeared again, but this time walked
to the edge of the ledge and appeared to push something over.

"I've got it!" said Grandfather. "She is cleaning out the nest.
Well, my lads, if we can find some way of getting to that spot,
within a week or two we will be in possession of some fine young
eyasses. Give her, say, a week from now to have cleaned up the nest
and laid her eggs, then another couple of weeks for the birds to
hatch and be ready to leave home, and that is where we step in."

"Hot dog!" said Joe with some enthusiasm.

"But we must not be too hasty. We must not do anything
that might cause the birds to desert their nest," said Grandfather
seriously. "We've got to explore the place and see if we can reach
the nest. If so, we can keep a check on the progress of the eyasses
and, at the right moment, secure them. If you like, we will have
a go at that tomorrow."

"Got to go to school." said Joe regretfully. "But of course we
can always play the wag, you know."

"I won't have that," said Mr. Mannering sternly. "You are
not going to play truant. We shall leave it until next Saturday."

"There is one good thing about all this," said David. "The
Christmas holidays are only a few weeks off and we'll have plenty
of time then to train our falcons."

"And you will need it," replied Grandfather darkly.

"What the heck will we do now?" asked Joe moodily. "It's too
early to go home. If we had some raw meat we could go fishing for
yabbies in O'Brien's waterhole. Anyway, let's go there. We might
find a dead fish or something. I've got a bit of string in my pocket."

As the waterhole lay more or less in the direction of home, Mr.

Mannering walked with the boys. O'Brien's waterhole had been dug out by the paddock's owner for the use of his stock and was roughly circular, with a diameter of about one hundred yards. As they approached it, a pair of indignant herons rose from the muddy edge with protesting croaks and wheeled lazily into the air. The waterhole was only half full and the hot sun, beating on to the drying mud at the sides, caused an aroma not exactly comparable with sweet violets, but that meant nothing to the lads, or Grandfather either. In any case he did not intend to linger there.

A cursory inspection of the mud did not reveal any dead fish, but as the trio got to windward of the mudhole, their noses were assailed by a particularly pungent scent.

"Something dead around these parts," said Joe unnecessarily.

"I can see it," said David in disgust. "Look over there—a dirty big dead eel."

The departed eel was six feet long and as thick as a man's arm. Mr. Mannering wrinkled his nose and intimated that he had no intention of remaining there a moment longer. Joe and David also developed a sudden yearning to be miles away from the place.

"Talking of eels," said Mr. Mannering as they walked along. "Where would you say that dead specimen was born?"

"In that stinking mudhole, I suppose," answered Joe. "It couldn't be anywhere else, unless it had wings."

"The life story of the eel," said Grandfather with the air of a lecturer, "is the strangest of all in the world of nature. That eel was not born in that waterhole at all. It was born in the sea, as all freshwater eels are."

"Hey!" exclaimed Joe. "Now, break it down a bit, Mr. Mannering. I mean to say, the sea must be all of sixty miles away from here. Do you mean to say that that eel, and all his cobbers, for the mudhole is full of them, came from the sea? Stone the beetles, you don't tell me that the things walked or crawled all this way?"

"That is exactly what I am telling you. It is true," said the old man. "The waterhole in this paddock is not a natural one. It was dug some years ago by Mr. O'Brien and he certainly did not put the eels in it. Neither did the birds carry them. They got here across country. The creek is only half a mile away and it runs into the river. That is how the eels got to the waterhole here. They were born probably thousands of miles away and they definitely were born in the sea, as all freshwater eels are."

Joe did not believe a word of it, but he did not say so.

As they walked along, Mr. Mannering told the two boys a most interesting story about eels which, in spite of Joe's private opinion, happened to be strictly true.

Freshwater eels in the rivers, creeks, waterholes, inland ditches and ponds of Australia, were all born somewhere in the warm seas north of the Commonwealth. When Mother Nature sent out the breeding call, the female eels heard and responded, because they must. From the waterholes, ponds, creeks and rivers, they headed for the sea. Travelling at night and slithering across the wet grass, using ruts and depressions where there was any water, or just dampness, they made their long and weary way instinctively to the nearest stream that would take them to the sea.

From all parts of the world the female eels migrated to their spawning grounds. These from the northern hemisphere—from England and other parts of Europe, America and such countries—made for the Sargasso Sea. Those from the southern hemisphere congregated north of Australia. But no matter where they came from, they sought the depths of the ocean, there to give life to millions of young eels, or elvers, and there to die; while the elvers made their slow and patient way back to where their mothers had spent most of their lives.

Newly-born elvers were just like small threads. It took them several years to cross the oceans again to the mouths of the rivers where their mothers had said a last farewell to land. For the female eels spawned only once in their lives. At the river mouths, the elvers concentrated in their millions for the comparatively shorter journey upstream. Of course, many stayed in the rivers. Many were content to live in the creeks; but there were the many hardy adventurers that, travelling by night as their mothers and fathers had done years before, made their way overland to the isolated waterholes, ponds, ditches and lagoons inland, there to live their lives until the call came to them in their turn to seek the sea, to spawn and to die. The males, of course, never migrated. They lived and died in their chosen waterholes, thousands of miles from the last resting place of their mates.

Of course, large numbers of elvers never had the chance to reach maturity. There were numerous hazards to overcome and enemies to elude in their thousands of miles' journey from their spawning place to their home water.

"And a good thing, too," wound up Grandfather with a smile. "Otherwise we would be overrun with eels."

CHAPTER NINE

Joe Goes Bird Nesting

THE expedition to the rocky eminence where they hoped to find the falcons' nest was undertaken on the following Saturday morning as planned. On the previous day, Grandfather, without telling the two boys of his intention, had made an excursion to the cliff, and from what he had seen, was convinced that the falcons had their nest in the crevice near where the gnarled tree jutted from the cliffside. He had then searched around until he had found an accessible scaling spot. This was a quarter of a mile away from the cliff face and provided a safe climb up the side of the ridge. Once on top, it was possible to thread one's way between rocks and scrub and trees to a point which actually overlooked the ledge fronting the nest crevice. Grandfather had been unable to climb down to the ledge, but he knew that, with the aid of ropes, it would be a simple matter for one of the boys.

His explorations had been watched with angry concern by both falcons. There were now three eggs in the nest and the birds were apprehensive of what the visit of this old human might portend. They had made no attempt to attack him, but they had kept a close check on his movements as they circled high above him.

On the Saturday expedition he took with him a long length of very strong rope and he explained to Joe and David exactly what he planned to do. They would go to the spot overlooking the nesting crevice and one of the boys would be lowered down by the rope. It was a drop of only about ten feet and there would not be the least danger. And immediately there occurred what

Grandfather had fully anticipated—a fierce argument as to who was going to make the descent.

"Toss for it and don't waste time," instructed Grandfather and David immediately produced a penny from his pocket.

"Give me a gander at that bronzer, it might be a doubleheader," said Joe nastily. "Hanged if I know why we have to toss. I'm a better climber than Dave is."

"Oh, shut up and toss the penny," said Grandfather. David did so. Joe called "heads" and "heads" it was.

Soaring high above the trees and rocks, Tiercel watched the three humans with anxious eyes. Black-cheek was on the nest in the crevice. He saw Grandfather tie one end of the rope around Joe's waist and the other round a convenient tree. Then the three humans lay down on their stomachs and examined the cliff face.

"It should be fairly easy going, Joe," said Mr. Mannering. "David and I will pay out the rope as you go down. There are plenty of outcrops for you to get footholds. Face the cliff, of course, and take it easy."

"All set," said Joe and, taking the rope in his hands, stepped backwards over the cliff edge. Grandfather and David slowly paid out the rope and Joe made easy but careful progress, successfully reaching the ledge, which was over two feet wide. Leaning over the edge and keeping a firm hand on the rope, Grandfather asked Joe what he could see. Joe shouted back that there was a hole in the rock face, but he could see nothing except a few sticks and twigs, which might be part of a nest.

Grandfather subjected the overhead sky and surrounding trees to a careful scrutiny but could see nothing of the adult falcons. He shouted this information to Joe, adding that he supposed both birds were away hunting.

But Mr. Mannering was wrong in this. Tiercel was perched on the limb of a tree not very far away, from where he could see everything that was going on. Black-cheek, of course, was on the nest. And she could see Joe, or part of him, though he couldn't see her.

Fearless to a degree though she was, the sight of this huge enemy—and Black-cheek knew instinctively that Joe was up to no good—scared the female falcon. But all she could do for the moment was to sit tight and await developments.

"I'm going to shove my hand in the crack and see if I can feel anything," Joe called out to Grandfather, who advised him to have a close look first. So Joe got down on his hands and knees and stared into the rock crevice. It was about three feet deep, but Joe did not know that. At first he could see nothing, the glare of the sun still being in his eyes, and then he made out a great heap of sticks and twigs and other material. Also, a hooked beak and a pair of shining eyes.

Black-cheek glared at him and he glared back. It would be hard to say which felt the most concern. They held this pose, boy and bird, for several seconds as if both were mutually hypnotised. Then Joe tore away his fascinated gaze and stood up.

"Hey, Mr. Mannering," he bawled out. "The old girl's on the nest."

"Do you mean the parent bird?"

"Yes. What will I do now?"

"Better leave her alone and come up here. She might desert the eggs if you go interfering with her."

"Say, what about Joe grabbing her?" suggested David excitedly. "We could train her all right. You said we could."

"Come down here and grab her yourself. You must think a man is a bit of a dill," snorted Joe.

"You had better come on up, Joe," said Mr. Mannering. "We'll hold the rope tight and you can walk up the cliff-side easily enough."

"Okay, here I come," Joe sang out. He took a firm grip on the rope and was about to gain his first foothold on the cliffside when he was knocked off his feet.

Black-cheek, brooding on her eggs and brooding in her mind upon the strange goings-on outside, had come to the conclusion that, though presence of mind was a virtue, absence of body had much to commend it also. She left the nest with a rush of wings, shot through Joe's legs and whirled aloft into the sky with a loud, defiant scream. The force of the impact sent Joe over the cliff and left him dangling in the air, clinging for dear life to the rope with frenzied hands. The rope was still secure around his waist, so there was not much fear of his falling to the hard rocks below; but that was small compensation for the terrific fright he got. Grandfather, who had witnessed the whole incident, gave a mighty heave on the rope and hauled Joe back on to the ledge, where he sat and trembled violently.

"Thought I was a corpse that time," he muttered.

"How are you, Joe?" bawled Grandfather. Joe replied that he had got his wind back and was ready to make the ascent.

"And I hope that that blessed bird doesn't have a crack at me while I'm doing it," he added. "Anyway, while I'm here I might as well see if there is anything in the nest."

Before he began his explorations, however, Joe had a good look at the skies, the bushes and the rocks. There was no sign of either falcon. Joe did not fancy a hooked beak in the back of his neck while he was down on his hands and knees.

Thrusting an arm into the crevice, Joe could just reach the nest. His questing fingers touched eggs and he counted three. They were quite warm. Promptly he rose to his feet and threw a fearfully-expectant glance at the heavens. Still no sign of the falcons.

"Three eggs in the nest," he shouted to David and Grandfather. "Now watch out. I'm coming up. Give me a haul and I'll be with you in two seconds."

Using every available toehold in the cliff face, and assisted by the united hauling efforts of Grandfather and David, he was with his companions on top of the cliff in no time.

"Three eggs, eh?" mused Grandfather. "We will have to keep a check on them. Let's get out of here as quickly as we can so that the mother bird will return. We can't run the risk of her deserting the nest. We can't do much now except wait. If the eggs are hatched, as soon as the eyasses are fledged, we will step in and take them prisoner. That won't be for a few weeks yet."

"Which will bring us nicely into the Christmas holidays," said David.

"Yes, and in the meantime we've got this silly school concert around our necks," gloomed Joe. "Why the heck do they have to have break-up concerts every year at school?"

"Don't you like concerts?" asked Grandfather.

"Oh, they're all right if you can just sit in the audience, but when you're expected to take part in them, it's not so hot. I'm no dashed actor, hang it."

"What have you got to do?"

"Don't know yet, but it's sure to be scaly. Old Emu-beak hasn't given us the bad news yet."

"And who," asked Grandfather curiously, "is old Emubeak?"

"Old Mitchell, the teacher," snorted Joe.

"That is not the way to talk about your school master," Grandfather reproved. "I've met Mr. Mitchell and he is a gentleman."

"Oh, he's all right, I suppose. Anyway, he has got a nose like an emu's beak," said Joe defiantly. "And if he wants to run concerts, why can't he hire decent artists instead of imposing on us?"

"Artists cost money," said Mr. Mannering.

"Exactly. And you can bet your boots that Emu-beak won't spend any if he can help it."

"But you have a Parents' and Citizens' Association attached to the school, haven't you?"

"Yes, and they encourage Emu-beak to hound us kids."

"I supose you never thought that Mr. Mitchell might use you children to discover if there is any talent among you? No, you wouldn't. And you had better not let him hear you call him Eagle's Beak, or there is likely to be ructions," said the old man.

"Emu-beak, not Eagle-beak," said Joe, who had a grievance. "Anyway, all the kids call him that, and all school teachers have nicknames. They mightn't think they have, but they'd be surprised, some of them, to hear what the kids call them."

"It is not respectful," said Grandfather.

"What did you call your teacher when you went to school in England?" demanded Joe.

"Er, that's a long, long time ago," said Mr. Mannering hastily. "I really forget now."

"I thought so," said Joe triumphantly. "That proves you called him something."

"Frogface," said Grandfather dreamily. "Yes, Frogface, and if ever a man had a face like a frog it was old Tom Montgomery."

"Bless my soul, how disrespectful!" said Joe gravely, and the three of them, man and boys, burst into hearty laughter.

CHAPTER TEN

Introducing Thunderbolt

IT'S hard; gosh, it's hard," commented Joe McKenzie gloomily, as he trudged home from school a few afternoons later in company with David and a school friend named George Eastwood. "Why have I got to be the mug all the time?"

"You're not on your own, cobber," said George. "We've all copped pretty crook jobs except Dave. He's sweet."

"How do you make that out, Botfly?" exclaimed David. "Haven't I got to sing in a trio with you and Joe?"

"Yes; but that finishes you off," said young Eastwood, who was known to his gentle and courteous playmates by the rather unattractive nickname of "Botfly." "What about Joe and me? We've got to stay behind the stage and work the silly curtain. Why can't old Emu-beak do it himself?"

"Because he wants to roam around the hall making a big feller of himself with the parents of the kids," said Joe bitterly. "It's going to be a first-class flop, this concert. Every item will be crook, even this song we three have to dish out. I can't sing for nuts and neither can you two mugs."

"You've said it," replied George, not the least offended.

"And isn't it going to be just lovely having to listen to that Aggie Herring trying to sing?" continued Joe. "Look, there is not a single person in this district who doesn't know that Aggie is the world's worst singer. She's dashed awful. But of course we know why she's on the programme—her old man is president of the Parents' and Citizens' Association and Emu-beak has to keep his marble good with him."

As may be guessed, the boys were discussing the forthcoming school concert. That day each pupil had been briefed in his or her part by the much-slandered Mr. Mitchell. That tireless worker was producer, director, stage manager, announcer and M.C. all rolled into one and would have scant leisure to hobnob with parents and citizens socially as Joe had insultingly suggested. He had to fill the programme somehow and though he knew full well that some of his artists were hopeless he had to do the best he could with the material on hand.

And he would have much preferred to leave Aggie Herring out of it. He knew she couldn't sing, but her name helped to fill the programme. Miss Herring was a sharp-featured miss of thirteen precocious years, who worked after school and at weekends as a spare waitress in her father's restaurant. Joe's description of her as "a nasty piece of homework" was a fair one. She was. In addition she was a mischievous young lady, a gossip and a pain in the neck.

George Eastwood parted company with the two chums at the corner nearest to his home and Joe and David walked on together. They left the township proper and plodded down a lane which led to a track along which their paths would diverge in opposite directions. Somebody was waiting for them at the intersection and as they got closer they saw that it was Grandfather Mannering.

"Hullo, boys," the old man hailed them cheerily. "I've got some news for you. I had a look in the falcon's nest this afternoon and two of the eggs have hatched out."

"Whacko! You beaut!" exclaimed Joe. "Now it won't be long."

"But how did you manage it, Grandfather?" David wanted to know. "Must have been stiff going for..." he broke off and reddened.

"For an old buffer like me, eh?" Mr. Mannering finished for him. He smiled broadly. "I'm not decrepit yet, David. It was very easy. I just tied the rope to a tree and lowered myself over the edge. I had a good look at the young birds. Strong healthy types that should make good hunters."

"How long will we have to wait now before we can take them away?"

"Three or four weeks at least."

"Gosh, as long as that?" Joe was disappointed. "Can't we take 'em now? We can feed 'em just as well as the old birds can."

"We can't and we are not going to try," said Grandfather. "Those birds are going to stay there until they are properly feathered. We are not going to rush this business. It is going to be done properly, or not at all."

"Okay, if you say so," said Joe sulkily. "Well, cheerio, I'll be seeing you." Saying which, he plodded off down the track while Grandfather and David also made their way home.

The next few weeks proved a restless and almost unhappy period for Joe. Concert rehearsals irked him and he was very discontented over the delay in commencing falcon-training. David did not worry. He was content to be guided wholly by Grandfather. Joe was not content, but he knew that if he did not do as he was told and leave the birds alone in the nest, Grandfather would abandon the whole idea.

One afternoon about four weeks after Grandfather had announced the hatching of two falcons' eggs, David and Joe again found the old man waiting for them as they plodded their way home from school. He was carrying a basket and as the boys approached they heard loud squawks of protest coming from it.

"Gosh, our hawks!" shouted Joe, breaking into a run. "Come on, Dave. Here's our blessed falcons at last!"

"All right, all right, fair go, give me a break!" exclaimed Mr. Mannering as the two excited boys mobbed him. "Hey, mind what you're doing, Joe, you clumsy young fool! Do you want to kill the eyas before she has her first lesson?"

He pushed the jubilant lad away and told him to calm down. Then carefully he lifted the lid of the basket. Inside Joe and David saw a well-fledged young falcon, which returned their eager stares with a fierce glare and a defiant squawk. Young as the eyas was, she was taking no cheek from anyone.

"Hey, Grandfather, you've only got one. Where's the rest?" cried Joe.

"Only two eggs hatched. The other is a tiercel. I told you before that the females are bigger and stronger and better to train. If we manage all right with one bird we'll be doing fine."

"Yes, but Dave and I want one each!"

"You'll take what you are getting and share the bird," said Mr. Mannering.

"Oh, all right. You're the boss," said Joe with a snort.

"See that you remember that as far as falconry is concerned," said Grandfather warningly.

The young falcon was established in a nest in a shallow box and placed on a shelf in a shed at the Burton home. All she was required to do for some time to come was to eat well and grow feathers. And she did both. It was necessary for Grandfather continually to warn Joe and David not to interfere. If they had had their way the eyas would have been killed with kindness and over-feeding.

"The bird has got to be kept hungry, but not starved," Mr. Mannering told them. "If she is, she will develop what are known as hunger-traces and she will never be any good."

Of course, Joe wanted to know what "hunger-traces" were and Grandfather had to explain that they were knife-like marks which appeared on the bird's feathers just where they joined the flesh. If the feathers broke, the falcon would not be able to fly properly.

"Thunderbolt," as Joe named her, grew fast and so did her feathers. She quickly developed colour—black on the head and cheeks, blue-grey on the back and white on the throat. Across her breast were the broad stripes that would turn into fine barrings as she grew older. She early became reconciled to her change of home and as long as meals were regular, she did not pine for her parents.

Mr. Mannering allowed both boys to handle her quite often

so that she would became used to them. He was always at pains to impress upon them that they had to be gentle with her. It was of major importance that they did not scare her by abrupt movements or rough handling. If this rule were not obeyed, she most likely would become timid and nervous. Thunderbolt, he said, was supposed to be a fierce bird of prey, if only a young one, and messing around and scaring her had to be avoided.

Joe confided to David that, in his considered opinion, Grandfather was a crank, a mug and an unnecessarily-strict crackpot; but David never wavered in his belief that Grandfather knew exactly what he was doing.

As Thunderbolt grew older, she was given an occasional mouse to eat and she heartily approved of the change from raw beef. One day Joe found a dead sparrow on his way home from school and gave her that. Thunderbolt accepted it and made a partial meal of it.

"Had it been alive and had she been allowed to kill it, she would have eaten the lot, bar the feathers, head and feet," said Mr. Mannering. "But that will come."

"Mean to say that we have to go and trap spadgers for her to kill and eat?" demanded Joe. "I'd rather catch mice. They're easier."

"It would be a good idea to have some mice by us," said the old man. "They are good eating for her. But she won't be trained to catch mice. We will have to let her kill birds during her training. It is most essential."

"Where are we going to get them from?" asked David.

"Sparrows are easy enough to catch in a trap with some seed or bread crumbs," said Mr. Mannering. "As for mice, Joe, if you can get some, we can keep them in a cage in the mews here and give them to Thunderbolt as needed."

"Keep 'em where?" asked Joe. "In the news?"

"I said mews, not news. Mews are places where falcons are kept in cages and trained. To mew also means to moult. It is an old English word. The real mews is an open space surrounded by hawks' cages. Many enclosed areas in London today are still called mews, dating from the days when they were used to train falcons. You've heard of the Royal Mews, haven't you? Well, today that is the place where the horses belonging to the Royal Family are kept and is on the exact site where, in ancient times, the kings of England trained their falcons."

"Yes, I see," said Joe. "All right then; I'll dig up a few mice and bring them along or give them to David. We can keep 'em in a cage here and feed 'em up fat. Higgins's store simply teems with mice and rats and I'll go there some time and collect a few."

"When can we start training Thunderbolt, Grandfather?" inquired David. "Soon now, eh?"

"Yes, within a week or so. I'll set to work to make a hood, a lure and the jesses. That should make you happy."

"Sure does," said David. "Everything is going along good-oh."

"Not everything," said Joe with a sudden scowl. "Don't forget that dashed school concert next Saturday night."

"Oh, gosh dam it!" moaned David in anguish.

CHAPTER ELEVEN

That School Concert

AND so the great night of the school concert arrived. David had arranged to meet Joe at a convenient street corner and go with him to the School of Arts hall. When he reached the rendezvous, Joe was already there and with him was George Eastwood. David noted, too, that Joe was carrying, wrapped up in brown paper, what appeared to be an oblong box.

"What's in the box, Joe, something to eat?" he asked.

"Eat, me foot!" replied Joe inelegantly. "I've got about two dozen mice in this box."

"Mice? What the heck are you taking mice to the concert for? Are you going to make a goat of yourself, putting on a trained animal act?"

"No, I'm not. Listen; I spent the best part of this morning catching these things in Higgins's feed store. They're for Thunderbolt and I'm not taking my eyes off them. I brought them along so that you could take them home with you tonight. If I left them at my place my mother would let them out."

David replied scathingly that the more sensible plan would have been for Joe to have taken the mice to the Burton home during the afternoon. The whole trouble with Joe was, David added, that he had no sense.

"Both you jokers have no sense, trying to train hawks," said George Eastwood. He was promptly told to close his face and keep it closed. Botfly's views did not matter a red cent to him, said Joe. He and David, if they chose, would train dragon flies or mosquitoes.

The School of Arts was a barnlike structure that had seen better days, but it was all the township had to offer in the theatre line. Joe, David and George went backstage on arrival, Joe still clutching his precious cargo of mice. These he managed to stow in an empty cupboard when nobody was looking. Backstage everything was in confusion. Agnes Herring, who, as Joe told her insultingly, had a hair-do that made her look like a millet broom in a fit, was practising her song in a corner, while Mr. Mitchell was instructing the orchestra—a man with a violin and the woman who would play the rickety piano—about the overture. Members of the Parents' and Citizens' Association dashed from point to point arranging this and that, while out in the hall members of the audience stamped their feet and whistled to each other.

Just before the curtain went up, Mr. Herring, as P. and C. president, appeared in in front of it and made an introductory speech. When he had finished, the piano and the violin struck up. They were off!

The first item was a recitation by a small girl who was just recovering from a bad cold and who was also in the throes of acute stage-fright. The audience listened impatiently to the few words they could hear and was obviously glad when the small girl finished and scuttled from the stage.

Second item was the Joe-David-Botfly singing trio. Their turn consisted of a song in which they marched on the stage in single file and sang a song as they walked in a circle. The number was called "Three Wise Old Men." Joe, who was clad in garments in which no self-respecting hunter would be seen dead, carried an old airgun. David had a small spade in his hand and was dressed in a coloured shirt with a pair of long pants tied with a bit of string under each knee, bowyang fashion. He was supposed to be a miner. George Eastwood had on his own clothes and over them wore his father's overcoat. Nobody knew what he was supposed to represent. They made an interesting trio. There were numerous verses to the song, the first and most important of which ran:—

"Three wise old men were they, were they,
Who went for a walk on a winter's day;
One carried a shovel to dig for gold,
One wore a big ulster to keep out the cold;
The third, and he was the wisest one—
To shoot the mosquitoes he carried a gun."

When the curtain went up, David with his spade marched on to the stage while Joe and George straggled after him like two lost sheep. They lined up and faced the audience, gibbering like frightened monkeys. Joe dug David in the ribs with his elbow and told him to start singing, for the love of Mike. David passed on the instruction to George, but none of the three obeyed.

"Sing, will you. Sing!" came a hoarse whisper offstage. Mr. Mitchell was becoming agitated.

With a strangled sob of despair, David commenced to circle the stage, followed by George in his overcoat and Joe bringing up the rear with his airgun. They circumnavigated the stage twice, the only sound coming from them being when David dropped his spade. He did not trouble to pick it up.

"WILL YOU SING!" roared Emu-beak in a voice that could be heard in every corner of the hall. "One carried a shovel to dig for gold'" David suddenly screamed in a high-pitched voice.

"Garn, you dropped it!" came a shout from the audience and everyone except Mr. Mitchell and the luckless trio on the stage laughed uproariously. Tears came into David's eyes, but he continued doggedly to march in a circle. Joe didn't. He lurched off the stage taking his gun with him. If any mosquitoes were to be shot, some other goat could shoot them. George, who wore his father's overcoat in lieu of the ulster called for in the song, followed Joe. It was mid-summer, not winter, and the overcoat made him feel hot.

"Get back on that stage and SING!" bellowed Emu-beak to the two deserters. David was now at a standstill in the centre of the stage, seemingly rooted to the floor. The audience hurled taunts and insults at him and advised him to go home. Mr. Mitchell, who had been working the curtain pending the release of George and Joe from their acting duties, let it down with a bang. David came out of his trance and dashed into the wings.

"I have not the time now to say to you three all that I desire to say," said Emu-beak, breathing hard. "You, Burton, may go and sit in the audience, or go home, or go to the devil. Eastwood and McKenzie will look after the curtain as previously arranged, and may heaven help them if they make a mess of things in any way."

Saying which, Emu-beak dashed in front of the curtain and announced a recitation by Henry McTavish. Henry came out and joined him and as soon as he had started imitating Harry Lauder, Emu-beak retired into a back room to calm down and regain his sanity.

The facilities at the School of Arts definitely were primitive. The curtain had to be hauled up by hand. To do this, Joe and George were housed in a little boxlike room at the side of the stage. There was a small opening for them to peer through to see what they were doing.

The curtain itself was made of venerable canvas and was kept down by a heavy pole nailed to the bottom. A foot of this pole was protruding from one end and artists who performed in front of the curtain were obliged to step over it to reach their positions.

Henry McTavish finished his recitation and was accorded some polite handclaps. He hopped over the protruding curtain-pole and disappeared. Mr. Mitchell then announced a conjuring turn, and as the whole stage was needed for this, he instructed George and Joe to raise the curtain and, after the act was over, to drop it and leave it down for Agnes Herring's song. While she was singing, arrangements for the next turn, which also would require the whole of the stage, would be carried out behind the curtain.

Joe and George raised the curtain without mishap for the conjuring turn and, while it was going on, Joe asked George to take care of things while he checked on his mice. He slipped out of the box and made his way to the cupboard. Nearby, David was talking to Agnes Herring. Joe examined the box and breathed a sigh of relief. Everything was in order.

"Hey, David," he said. "if you're going down into the audience, will you take these mice and mind them? I don't think they're safe here."

"No, I won't," said David instantly. "I don't want to be saddled with a box of mice. I'm going home, anyway. I've had this concert."

"Well, take 'em home with you."

"I won't!" said David.

"What are you doing with mice in a box?" demanded the inquisitive Aggie.

"Mind your own business," said Joe shortly. "They're not for your old man to put in his meat pies, anyway."

"I don't believe you've got mice in the box," said Aggie with a toss of the head.

"No. They're heliotrope wombats," said Joe, telling a lie.

"You two are going to cop it," said Aggie nastily. "I hope old Mitchell half-kills you. And I'll tell my father what you said about putting mice in his meat pies."

"Thanks," said Joe. "Now get out there and sing. It's your turn. Heaven help the poor old audience!"

Aggie darted him a look filled with venom but there was no time for her to indulge in more than looks. The conjuring act was over and George Eastwood had dropped the curtain as instructed. Aggie marched across the stage and was in the act of stepping across the piece of protruding pole when George, who was brooding over the fact that Joe had left him to do all the work, forgot his instructions and began frantically to haul up the curtain. He caught Aggie properly.

As he hauled, Aggie screamed, and no wonder. George was rolling her up in the curtain! He lifted her three feet from the floor before he woke up, and then he left the curtain drop with a crash. The audience howled and whistled with delight. They loved the little unrehearsed incident.

Aggie Herring was made of very determined material. Picking herself up and grinding her teeth with rage, she strode in front of the curtain and faced the audience, her hands on her hips.

"Listen to me, you laughing hyenas," she shouted. "You think you're funny, don't you? Well, you are not! I'm going to sing if I stay here all night, see?"

More roars of mirth, feet stamping and whistling. The audience loved Aggie. Her father didn't. He sketched out in his mind exactly what he would say and do to her when he got her home after the concert. Backstage, Emu-beak Mitchell was also planning what he intended to do to her, as well as to Joe, George and David, at the first opportunity.

Disdaining further comment, Aggie signalled to the piano and violin and then opened her mouth to sing.

"Steak and kidney pie!" shouted somebody in the sixth row. Aggie closed her mouth like a rabbit trap. For three seconds she played her eyes like searchlights around the hall, trying to locate the offender. Then she opened her mouth again.

"Lamb and mint sauce!" bellowed a voice from the back of the hall.

"Ice cream, sixpence a lump; the more you eat, the more you jump!" came floating in a childish treble from a far corner.

"What price steak and oysters?" yelled somebody else, while others screamed their derision and made insulting remarks about Aggie's spare-time occupation of waitress in a cafe.

Miss Herring was attempting to pinpoint the insulters when she was joined by Mr. Mitchll, who made a short and pungent address in which he laid stress on the lack of manners apparent in the audience. If there was any more of it, he said, the concert would come to a full stop. He then retired and Aggie once more had the centre of the stage.

She threw one long, venomous glare around the hall and then signalled to the orchestra. And when the first shattering notes of her song rent the air, all else was mute. It had to be. Aggie's voice brooked no rivals in the great world of pandemonium. She was not a large girl, but her nerveshattering voice filled the hall and went echoing up the street outside.

While she was singing, Joe rejoined George and advised him to be a bit more careful when he was rolling up curtains.

Aggie finished her song amid stunned silence and, without waiting for any applause, gave a very stiff and very formal bow and marched off the stage, warily avoiding the protruding pole, breathing threats and slaughter. Striding into the small room, she faced George with blazing eyes.

"Do you think I'm an acrobat, you numbskull?" she hissed.

"Wasn't me, was him," said George with great presence of mind, pointing at Joe. "He did it, not me."

"Is that so? I might have known it. Him and his mice! Funny fellow, ain't he? Likes his little joke. I'll fix him!"

She glared at the speechless Joe for a second and then resumed her tongue-lashing. "Trying to make a goat of me in front of the audience. I'll fix you, Joe McKenzie. Try this for size." Saying which, she deliberately smacked Joe on the right ear with a force that made his head spin round.

"Hey, that hurt, Aggie!" bellowed Joe in pain. "You silly fool.

It was Botfly who wound you up in the curtain, not me. Don't you remember me being over the other side of the stage with you and Dave Burton when you got your call?"

"Hey? Yes, I remember," she breathed, turning suddenly on the grinning George. His grin vanished like magic when she doubled her fist and punched him on the nose. Without deigning to apologise to Joe, she tossed her head and marched off the stage to the dressing room.

The next few turns went off without a hitch and then the interval arrived. Joe immediately rushed off to the cupboard to check up on his mice. But when he opened the door of the cupboard he found, to his horror and dismay, that the box was missing. He could not believe his eyes. There was nothing in the cupboard but dust and dead moths. The box could not have walked away, so somebody must have taken it.

"Who pinched my mice?" he howled to high heaven. Nobody answered, because there was nobody around. Being intermission, almost everyone was outside the hall getting a breath of fresh air. One exception was George, who was fooling around in the curtain-raiser's box.

"More fool you for bringing them here," said George unsympathetically when Joe poured out his tale of woe. "Anyway, who would want to get down on a box of mice? They must be somewhere around."

"They're gone, I tell you!" roared Joe in anguish. "Two dozen mice that I spent all that time catching for my falcon."

"Well, go and catch some more."

"Break it down. It took me hours to catch that lot. Gosh, I wish I knew the joker who pinched them. I'd make him smart for it."

"Where's Dave Burton? Maybe he's got them," suggested George. "He said he was going home, so he must have taken them with him."

"By gosh, Botfly, so he might have," exclaimed Joe, clutching at straws. "Yes, I guess he did. I brought them here for him to take home. Whacko! Gee whizz! That's a weight off my mind, by heck!"

Down in the audience sat Miss Agnes Herring with a malicious grin on her face. She'd teach that Joe McKenzie to say insulting things about the quality of the pies served in her father's cafe. She looked speculatively at the brown paper parcel on her lap. She had no idea why Joe McKenzie should collect a lot of mice but they apparently were very valuable in his eyes. That was why she had extracted them from the cupboard. If she let them go it would be a sweet revenge on the McKenzie lad.

So Aggie, who, unlike a lot of girls, was not in the least afraid of mice, now sat in the audience at the side of a female acquaintance with the picturesque name of Hortense Harcourt and chuckled to herself.

"Know what's in this box, Hortense?" she said. Hortense replied that she hadn't the foggiest notion.

"Mice," said Aggie briefly.

"Did you say mice?" ejaculated Hortense, recoiling from her in terror.

"Yes, and if you make any wisecracks about them being for the meat pies my father makes, I'll belt you until you can't stand up straight," said Aggie darkly.

"Gee, Aggie, I never thought of saying such a thing," Hortense assured her. Then, in reply to questions, Aggie informed her how she had become possessed of the mice. As to what she intended to do with them now she had them, she had no idea at the moment.

"Unless I let them loose in this hall and cause a bit of a stir," she said dreamily.

"You wouldn't do that, would you, Aggie?" howled Hortense.

"Wouldn't I just!" replied Aggie with a meaning chuckle and Hortense, who knew that Aggie was capable of almost anything, muttered something about wanting to see her mother, got up from her seat and left the hall at a run.

Aggie, a curious smile on her face, watched Hortense's rapid departure, and then concentrated her attention on the stage. The lights had gone out and the small orchestra was playing the overture to the second half of the programme. There were three other people sitting on the same long form as Aggie, but not close to her. Slowly and carefully she untied the string around the box and took off the brown paper. The box was of cardboard and at some time had housed a pair of large boots. Placing it on the floor unobserved, she silently lifted the lid and slid it back a little. Then she gave the box a deft kick which sent it sliding six feet towards the stage. It came to rest under a form three rows in front of where she sat. Aggie folded her arms and sat back to await developments. They were not long in coming.

Suddenly there was a scream like a train whistle as a fat old lady left her seat with one mighty, upward leap. Announcing in a shrill voice that her legs were being chewed off by scorpions, she waddled rapidly towards the exit. From all parts of the hall squeals and howls announced that other people were having trouble. An old man shouted out something about it raining trapdoor spiders and made a great effort to extract a wandering mouse from up his trouser leg. A young girl, who leaped on to a seat with a squeal, trod on the old man's best hat and this made him complain some more. There was a terrific din which drowned out the feeble, competing efforts of the violin and piano, which soon gave it up as a bad job.

Joe had said that there were two dozen mice in the boot box. People in the audience would have sworn that there must have been over two hundred. The commotion caused Mr. Mitchell to switch on all the lights and the astonished observers thought that the hall was alive with mice. They were running up the slanting side beams, crawling along the rafters and tearing across the floor.

Joe, backstage, hearing the uproar, dashed in front of the curtain. Mice! Where did they come from? Surely they were not his? Hadn't David taken the box home after all? He was wringing his hands in anguish when he was joined by Mr. Mitchell.

"What is all this terrific noise about, McKenzie?" he yelled to make himself heard above the general tumult.

"Mice," Joe yelled back. "The hall is full of mice. Somebody must have let mine out of their box."

Mr. Mitchell did not understand him, but he shouted to the audience to calm down. There were not too many now to shout at because the mouse invasion was effectually clearing the hall. Except for a few venturesome boys who were treating the whole affair as a gigantic lark and were busy chasing the mice around the place, the hall was soon emptied and eventually peace was restored.

"And now, McKenzie, perhaps you can enlighten me as to what has been going on," said Mr. Mitchell with cold hostility.

"Some coot let my mice out," howled Joe.

"I am not very good at riddles, McKenzie," said the teacher. "Tell me exactly what you are talking about."

Still wringing his hands, Joe explained about the falcon and the mice and how David was to have taken them home with him. But some hidden hand had taken them and let them loose in the hall.

"I think that is one of the most fantastic stories I have ever heard, McKenzie," said Mr. Mitchell. "You boys all think I am a fool. Maybe I am—but I'm not that silly. This concert has been completely ruined, mostly by your efforts and those of Agnes Herring. I shall deal with you both most severely at school on Monday."

Aggie Herring! A great light broke upon Joe. Aggie! Of course! She knew all about the mice. He did not mention his suspicions to Emu-beak. He would deal with her himself. And in the meantime his beloved Thunderbolt would starve.

"I shall see you at school on Monday, McKenzie," said Emu-beak. "I'm afraid I won't be there, sir," said Joe quietly.

"Oh, and why not?" exclaimed the astonished teacher.

"You forget, sir," replied Joe dreamily. "We broke up yesterday for the Christmas holidays. Remember?"

CHAPTER TWELVE

"Burton Mews"

WHEN Grandfather went into the shed one morning to feed Thunderbolt and found that young falcon had left the nest and was hopping around on the shelf, he judged that it was time to commence her training. He decided to wait until Joe turned up so that the boy would miss nothing. Joe was sure to be there the first thing after breakfast. In fact, he spent so much time now at the Burton home that his mother had advised him sarcastically to take his bed over and sleep in the shed with his precious falcon.

Grandfather had made the jesses—the thin strong leather straps about six inches long and these he tied to Thunderbolt's legs. The young falcon, they found by experiment, was able to fly a little, so Mr. Mannering said that henceforth she would be tied down to the feeding platform in case she took a fancy to leave them.

And so the training of Thunderbolt began. Grandfather attended to her feeding and David and Joe took it in turns to have her sit on their wrists. They wore gloves to prevent scratches from her sharp talons. In this way the bird became familiar with both lads. She already treated Grandfather as an old friend because of his daily feeding of her.

Thunderbolt's food nowadays was given to her on the lure. As neither Joe nor David could be persuaded to go and shoot a bird so that its wings could be used as part of this lure, Grandfather had compromised by manufacturing an ingenious affair out of a padded horseshoe, around the edges of which he stuck feathers from the fowlyard. Thunderbolt at first did not take kindly to wearing the hood, but she could not get out of it—in two ways. Eventually, however, she became reconciled to the annoying affair.

There was great excitement at "Burton Mews," as David had named the training yard, when the lure was used for the first time. David had Thunderbolt perched on his wrist and Joe held the lure with a piece of raw meat on it, a few feet away. It was five minutes before the falcon would consent to leave David's wrist and hop across to Joe's, but when she did so and was rewarded with a piece of the meat, the first round of the battle had been won.

Day after day the old man and the two boys trained the young falcon. They always had a long string tied to the jesses to make certain that she did not take it into her head to go walkabout, or, rather, flyabout. When she had learned to fly a full hundred yards to the lure to gain a meal, Mr. Mannering judged that it was time to enter her at a live bird. He suggested that they should trap a sparrow for the purpose. Joe offered to catch it. David did not fancy the idea at all.

"It doesn't seem right," he said. "I'm beginning to change my mind about this falconry business. It is quite natural for a wild hawk to hunt down birds to kill and eat, for that is the way of the species; but for us people to train a falcon to hunt birds for our own fun is a bit over the odds."

"You feeling sick or something, Dave?" inquired Joe anxiously.

David replied that the only sickness he felt was over the need to catch a live sparrow for Thunderbolt to kill without the sparrow having a chance.

"Getting soft-hearted all of a sudden, eh?" jeered Joe.

"Not so soft-hearted that I can't belt the ears off you any time I feel like it," retorted David spiritedly.

"Break it up, boys, and don't let us have any brawls," said Mr. Mannering. "I can appreciate David's viewpoint. But, lad," he added kindly, "how do you expect us to train a falcon if we miss one of the most important lessons?"

"As far as I am concerned," the boy replied steadily, "I don't care if we give up the whole jolly idea."

"Aw, nuts!" said Joe. "I'll get the sparrow, Mr. Mannering."

It was a red-letter day when Thunderbolt, her training over, was taken into O'Brien's paddock for her first stoop at a wild bird. By now she would readily return to the lure when she was hungry. That had been proved when first she was allowed to fly at hack—her initial lease of freedom from the restricting line on the jesses. Joe was now head falconer. David would have nothing to do with it. Grandfather was a kind of emergency. Thunderbolt would return to either of them.

The falcon's debut as a hunting hawk proved something of a fiasco. Grandfather, David and Joe, with the bird on the latter's wrist, went to O'Brien's paddock and after walking around for perhaps five minutes without seeing any worthwhile game, they sighted a peewit. Now, peewits are notoriously poor fliers, and for a pergrine facon to attack one was akin to an R.A.A.F. jet fighter taking on an Aero Club training 'plane. An experienced falcon would merely have dropped from the skies on top of the peewit and murdered it with one swift stroke.

When the peewit came flapping clumsily over the treetops, Joe quickly undid the jesses.

"No," said Grandfather quickly. "Don't enter her at such a tame quarry. Joe. Wait until something better turns up."

But it was too late. Thunderbolt was already in the air. She looked around to see what she was supposd to tackle and saw the peewit. But instead of circling high to get above the quarry and then stooping, she shot straight from Joe's wrist at the startled black and white bird.

The peewit saw the falcon coming and, with a loud screech, made for a big gum tree only a few yards away. Thunderbolt shot after it and had almost reached it, when from out of the tree darted a small black and white bird with an absurdly long tail. Straight at

Thunderbolt dived Willy Wagtail, snapping with his ineffectual beak and screeching like a bad-tempered witch. Disconcerted by this attack, Thunderbolt did not watch where she was going, and crashed into the tree trunk. The peewit flew through some bushes and escaped, while Willy Wagtail, no doubt considering that he had done his good deed for that day by assisting his peewit pal, darted off across the paddock in the direction of the creek.

Thunderbolt, now minus a few feathers, managed to reach a limb of the tree. There she preened herself a little and then lapsed into deep thought. At last Joe managed to attract her attention by swinging the lure. Habit made her glide down from the tree and take her seat on the boy's outstretched wrist.

"Don't be disheartened. She will learn," said Grandfather. "She is very inexperienced. Remember, Thunderbolt is man-trained, not nature-trained. She has everything to learn, but will improve, and fast."

And improve she did. As the days and weeks fled, the falcon became a deadly hunter, bringing down all kinds of birds. She even learned a few tricks of her own.

Thunderbolt readily took to rabbit hunting. It was unnecessary for Joe or Grandfather to spot one for her. They would take her out into the paddocks and loose her. Thunderbolt would circle the area until she saw a rabbit and then stoop like lightning. On one occasion her quarry reached its burrow only a few inches ahead of her and she tried to follow it. Joe had to drag her out, but she left a few feathers in the burrow mouth as a reminder to the rabbits of the perils of the great big world of hawks and men.

As time wore on, she became very cunning with rabbits. Sometimes she would stalk them, flying from tree to tree until the quarry began feeding in an open space. Unaware of the peril from the skies, the rabbit never knew what struck it down.

David accompanied Joe on one or two of the hawking trips, but Grandfather, as soon as he was satisfied that Thunderbolt had no more to learn, left the boys to themselves. He told himself whimsically, that he would be definitely the last of the Mannering falconers. David had little interest in the sport, thinking it cruel; but it was no worse than live-hare coursing with greyhounds. He told David that in falconry the quarry had more than a fifty-fifty chance, but David was unconvinced.

Thus it was that Joe, now a most devoted hawker, often went out alone, returning on every occasion with stories of Thunderbolt's truly remarkable prowess in the field. One day he returned with a black eye which, he said, had been given to him, while he wasn't looking, by Botfly Eastwood. Botfly, Joe added grimly, had gone home on a stretcher.

Pressed for details, Joe said that Botfly had been flying his model aeroplane in the paddock and Thunderbolt, taking it for some kind of bird, had stooped on it from a great height and completely wrecked it.

"Model Aero Clubs often have that trouble with wild hawks," said Grandfather with a great laugh. "Their members are continually complaining about it."

But Thunderbolt was indeed an efficient hunter. She had now added to her human-imparted education the natural hunting instincts inborn in her and handed down through a long line of predatory falcons.

One day Joe issued a special invitation to David and Grandfather to cross the creek with him to Jackson's slaughterhouse and watch Thunderbolt hunt crows. They accepted the invitation.

"She's got crow-hunting down to a fine art," said the enthusiastic Joe as the three of them set forth. "You haven't seen her in action for some time. Today you're gonna see something extra-special."

Thunderbolt, perched on Joe's wrist and tied down with the jesses, uttered a complacent squawk as if she fully endorsed Joe's testimonial.

When they got near the slaughterhouse paddock, Joe loosed

her. As a preliminary, the falcon skimmed along a few feet above the ground and then gradually began to rise in a long, sweeping circle. Up and up she went, and as the three friends watched, she perched on the topmost branch of a gigantic blue gum. Here for a moment she idly preened her feathers and then took stock of her surroundings.

Presently, from away across the paddock there floated the mournful "kark, kark, kark" of a crow. This was answered from still further away by an equally melancholy "far-ther, far-ther" as another bush undertaker took up the dirge. The sad chorus was like a clarion call to Thunderbolt. Taking off from the tree, she circled over Joe's head, spiralling higher and higher.

"We will stay here for a bit," Joe told his companions. "This is where we have downed quite a few crows. They make a habit of flying across this open spot. Thunderbolt will stay up there until she sees one. Then you'll see something yourselves."

In spite of his recently-acquired aversion to hawking, David was as interested as Joe, while Grandfather beamed with pride. After all, it was he who had trained Thunderbolt.

"Ah!" exclaimed Joe suddenly. "Here comes one of the black coots. Now we'll get a bit of action. Watch!"

Grandfather and David watched, fascinated, as a black blob floated towards them. The crow was perhaps two hundred feet up and if it maintained its present course, would fly directly over their heads.

"Keep as still as you can. You know what crows are. It might change its course if it sights us," said the experienced Joe.

The crow did maintain its course and when it was almost overhead, the human watchers thought that Thunderbolt had missed it. She hadn't. As they watched enthralled, they saw the high-circling falcon suddenly tip over sideways and drop earthwards. Down she came at a terrific speed in a perfectly perpendicular plunge. And as she came, they noticed that her wings were half-shut, her feet were straight back, and her tail closed tight. Occasionally she seemed to give a few short beats with her wings, and this, if anything, increased a speed that already was almost unbelievable.

And so quickly did Thunderbolt hurtle earthwards that it looked as if a small dot had suddenly developed into a huge ball-a ball that resolved itself into a savage killer.

Thirty feet above the crow, Thunderbolt screamed harshly. The crow heard her and made a dash for the trees. He had no chance at all, for, before he could add another yard to his flight, the falcon had struck him on the head and had shot upwards again. Circling round, she watched the stricken black bird tumbling over and over, shedding sable feathers which zigzagged to earth. Then, tipping over once more, she shot to the ground and was standing there when the crow landed. With another scream, Thunderbolt hopped upon the dead body and stood there a little contemptuously, staring at Joe.

"Good on you, you little beauty!" exclaimed the boy as he held out his arm. With some reluctance, Thunderbolt left the crow and fluttered to his gloved hand. Joe immediately gave her a piece of meat.

"Well, what do you think of her now, hey?" he said proudly, as he stroked the falcon's sleek head.

"Magnificent, my boy," applauded Grandfather. "I'll wager that no knight of old had a better trained peregrine. I've seen a bit of hawking in the Old Country, but none better than Thunderbolt and that crow."

"Sir Joseph McKenzie, at your service," said Joe with a bow.

David, who had been standing silently and staring at the dead crow, turned to Grandfather, a frown on his face.

"I thought you said that the quarry had more than a fifty-fifty chance?" he asked. "That crow had no chance at all. Even when Thunderbolt screamed, she was travelled so fast that the crow couldn't get away."

"It would have been just the same if Thunderbolt had been a wild falcon out hunting. Who cares about a crow anyway?" said Joe. "They're useless things, picking the eyes out of sheep and so on."

"That's not the point at all," said David. "Anyway, we won't brawl about it, but you can count me out of hawking in the future."

"You wouldn't have lasted long in the days of my old pal Edward the Third," said Joe scoffingly. "You'd be shoved in some dungeon for running down the sport of kings."

"Sir Joseph McKenzie, the gallant and gentle knight," said David, and his tones were most insulting. Grandfather sensed trouble between the two lads, trouble that might lead from mere words to hard blows. He was about to interpose some soothing observations when Thunderbolt, whom Joe had forgotten to secure to his wrist with the jesses, suddenly took off and soared leisurely into the blue.

"What is she after now, I wonder?" asked Joe as he watched the graceful ascent. "There isn't a bird in the sky."

"Oh, she's just having a bit of exercise," said Grandfather. "Let us start walking. We might flush something for her."

With Joe at his side and the reluctant David a pace or two behind, Grandfather strolled off. High above, Thunderbolt saw them moving and widened her circling. Coming to the fence that separated O'Brien's paddock from the slaughterhouse property, they crawled through and as Joe straightened himself up, he stumbled over a big tuft of grass. From right under his feet, seemingly, a terrified brown lark dashed and hurled itself into the air. Joe pulled aside the grass tuft and discovered a cup-shaped nest of dried grass containing three salmon-pink eggs speckled at the larger end.

"Nearly squashed the blessed thing," Joe observed and then glanced upwards to see what Thunderbolt was doing. She was still high above, a large dot against the brazen blue of the sky. And far below her Joe saw the lark he had flushed. It was spiralling upwards and singing melodiously, despite the fact that, not a minute earlier, it had had the wits scared out of it by a clumsy, big-footed boy. Ceasing its upward flight, the lark hovered on trembling wing perhaps fifty feet above their heads and then the watchers saw something else—the mighty Thunderbolt in her killing dive.

The lark, whose hovering was the usual preface to a return to earth, began to drop. She did not know of the menace above her.

Then, all at once, the whistling and whining sound of the plunging falcon's feathers reached her highly-sensitive ears. With a desperate "chirp-chirp-chirp" of pure terror, the little brown bird, a fast flier in her own right, shot towards the ground. She had a fairly long start on the falcon, but Thunderbolt was a screaming terror on wings. Down swept the lark, and down rushed the falcon, only a few yards separating them as they reached the watching human trio.

The desperately-terrified lark could find no sanctuary. The paddock hereabouts was bare. There was not a single tree or bush within easy distance. Its small heart near to bursting point, its little beak gaping open and its eyes dilated with pure horror, it suddenly banked and flew straight at Joe.

And with Thunderbolt's great hooked beak close enough to rip out its tail feathers, the little brown lark dived frantically into Joe's open shirt front and wriggled right up under his right armpit. The falcon, unable to pull out of her jetlike plunge, hit the boy smack on the chest, knocking him over backwards. Down he went and, luckily, fell upon his left side. The lark was under his right arm. Thunderbolt was now clutching his shirt front, but with the disappearance of her small quarry, she had lost interest in it. She disentangled her talons from Joe's torn shirt and threw herself into the air. And when she saw Grandfather's outstretched hand, she flew obediently to it and sat there, her claws digging into his flesh. Grandfather was not gloved like Joe and the bird's talons hurt.

With a grunt he jerked his hand upwards and the surprised falcon found herself in the air. For a moment she flew uncertainly low down and then soared away up high, presently to resume the everlasting hunting circle.

Joe had now risen to his feet and on his face there was a most peculiar look. Gingerly he thrust his left hand into his shirt and felt under his right armpit. His fingers touched a small, palpitating ball of feathers and very gently he brushed it down until it rested on top of his belt. For a moment or two he could not speak. Both Grandfather and David, too, were silent.

"It's a good job I'm not ticklish or I would have squashed the little fellow," said Joe dazedly, and lapsed into silence. Then, "What do you know about that?" he said very slowly and thoughtfully. "Fancy that little lark coming to ME of all persons, for protection. And from MY falcon. Gee whizz; you wouldn't read about it!"

"It has happened many times," said Grandfather, as Joe again lapsed into a bewildered silence. "There are numerous instances of birds taking refuge with people to get away from a more deadly foe."

"But what could be more deadly to a bird than a boy?" asked David soberly. "Boys kill more birds than anyone. I've done a lot myself."

"Stone the beetles. Who would have thought it?" came from Joe, who was really talking to himself. "Coming to ME for protection."

"Well, Sir Joseph, aren't you going to give it to Thunderbolt to finish off?" asked David maliciously.

"What?" roared Joe indignantly. "You must think I'm a pretty rotten sort of joker to do that after the little feller came to me for protection." He broke off and brooded intensely. "I tell you what I'm going to do. I'm going to give the lark to you and you're going to stop right here with it until Thunderbolt and I are out of sight. Then you can let the lark go."

"I'll do that like a shot, Sir Joseph," said David.

"Oh, cut that out!" exclaimed Joe. Very carefully and gently he withdrew the small bird from his shirt and handed it over to David. The lark was still trembling with fright. Being wholly at the mercy of a small boy, it did not know how long it had to live.

A glance upwards showed Joe that the graceful Thunderbolt was still describing the hunting circle; so, accompanied by Grandfather, he made his way quickly across O'Brien's paddock. The falcon noted the move and followed him. It was not until all danger of her seeing the lark had passed that David opened his hand. For a moment the small creature just lay quietly in his open palm. The boy gave a gentle hand jerk and the little bird, coming suddenly to life, darted away and dived into a dense patch of grass.

When David arrived at "Burton Mews," there was no sign of Joe. Grandfather told him that Thunderbolt was safe in her quarters and that Joe had gone home, still babbling about the wonder of the lark's desperate bid for a haven.

"And do you know what?" Mr. Mannering said thoughtfully. "I am inclined to think that Joe's hawking days are numbered. I have never seen a lad so upset as he was over that lark episode. Although he did not put it into so many words, he gave me the impression that he now sees himself as the protector of little birds. He cannot be that and a falconer too."

"I do wish he'd chuck it up," said David. "But supposing we did let Thunderbolt go, how do you think she would get on in the bush?"

"David," Grandfather said, "Thunderbolt is a well-trained killer. Hitherto she has not eaten any of her kills because either Joe or I have always been handy to feed her from the lure. If she killed something and we were not handy, hunger would provide the necessary incentive for her to follow her natural instincts and make a meal. No, Thunderbolt would never starve."

It was three whole days before Joe again visited "Burton Mews." He sought out Grandfather and told him that he was giving up hawking. If Grandfather and David did not object, he would return Thunderbolt to the bush, the mountains and the plains, there to live her own life as Nature had intended.

Grandfather assured the boy that he did not object in the least. It had been, he said, a most interesting experiment and he was quite satisfied. He had no desire to continue hawking with the falcon. David echoed his words.

"I'm glad you're doing it, Joe," he said simply, and held out his hand. Joe grinned faintly and shook it heartily.

"I would suggest, Joe, that you take Thunderbolt some distance away from these parts and free her just on dusk so that she will have a night in the bush in strange surroundings. Next day she will awake in new country and, being naturally hungry, will commence hunting instinctively. She will soon forget her human companions."

"That is how I worked it out myself," nodded Joe. "It's mighty hard to part with the old girl, but when I think of that little lark .... What I'm going to do, Mr. Mannering, is to put her in a cage and take her in the train about twenty miles down the line. I'll let her go there just on dusk with a good feed under her belt to see her through the night. I'll keep out of sight in the station until the train comes back in."

"An excellent plan," applauded Grandfather.

"Good on you, Joe!" said David.

"Okay then," said Joe. "I'll do it tomorrow."

And he did.

THE END